ACCRUALS ACCOUNTING
IN THE PUBLIC SECTOR

Forthcoming titles in the public sector management series

Accruals accounting in the public sector

by
Valerie Archibald

Published by Longman in association with
The Civil Service College.

ACCRUALS ACCOUNTING IN THE PUBLIC SECTOR

Published by Longman Information and Reference, Longman Group Ltd, 6th Floor, Westgate House, The High, Harlow Essex CM20 IYR, England and Associated Companies throughout the world.

A catalogue record for this book is available from The British Library

ISBN 0–582–23894–3

Printed and bound in Great Britain by Bookcraft (Bath) Ltd.

Contents

Series foreword

The Longman/Civil Service College series of texts on Management in the Public Sector covers many of the most important topics on the current management agenda, in central government and in the public sector as a whole. In the past many of these topics may have been the preserve of specialists. Finance was for Finance Division, human resource issues were for the Personnel Group, contracts were Contracts Branch. Increasingly all managers, at senior, middle and junior management levels, find themselves drawn into these, previously specialist, topics. With flatter management structures and increased delegation, all managers need a broad understanding of a range of management topics. This series of books has been produced with their needs in mind.

The texts are intended to be straightforward to understand, to provide a good summary of current understanding and best practice, and to illustrate the key points with examples from the public sector. There will still be room for the specialist, but these texts should enable every manager to talk intelligently with the specialist and understand him or her better.

This particular text is especially timely, coinciding with the development of resource accounting in central government. Accruals accounting will be an important element of resource accounting. The Civil Service College's own experience of accruals accounting has shown that the basic principles need to be understood throughout the organisation. It affects everyone involved in any way with financial transactions and accounting for them. It is hoped that this text will help all such people to understand more clearly how and why accruals accounting affects them.

I would like to thank Bob Pike and Alison Graham for their sterling efforts to prepare the printed texts for this series. I hope that you will find this and all of the other texts helpful.

Robert J. Smith

July 1994

Author's foreword

I have written this book with a particular type of person in mind as the reader. This person needs to understand the principles of accruals accounting, and how they are applied in the public sector, to help them make sense of the accounts that are being produced.

This book is designed to give the reader a sound, basic understanding. It will not turn the reader into an expert - several years' professional training and experience would be needed! It will equip them to ask questions of appropriate experts and to understand the answers they are given.

I have received much help in the reasearch and preparation of this book. My thanks go to Ken Bradley, Chris Butler, Graham Gilmour, Peter Hall, Chris Richards, and David Wellard of HM Treasury, Harry Wilkinson of the Audit Commission, Paul Humfryes of the Department for Education and Chris Wilson of CIPFA. Thanks also go to copyright owners for permission to quote their material, particularly to Chapman and Hall, Surrey County Council, the Post Office, British Coal, and the Hanover Housing Association.

At the Civil Service College, I wish to thank colleagues among the teaching staff and librarians, as well as the many individuals from other organisations who I have learnt from as well as taught.

I thank my husband, for acting as the intelligent layman, and reading through the text to make sure it made sense.

And finally, there are those who have helped, but wished not to be named. Thank you to those also.

Any errors which remain are my own, and I would be grateful if these could be drawn to my attention. The topic is fast evolving, and a second edition is very likely.

Valerie Archibald

Sunningdale

Chapter 1

The need for accruals accounting

> The additional benefits which accrual accounting can provide for public sector entities include the ability to: reflect and provide the basis for accountability for the additional flexibility provided to public sector managers; underpin objectives for a more competitive approach to public sector provision; facilitate more efficient and effective resource management; improve accountability by extending the notion of performance beyond the use and application of cash; and provide a longer term focus on the effect of government and management decisions (OECD, 1993)

Cash accounting is very much the tradition in central government. In the United Kingdom, it has been used as the prime basis for Parliamentary control over the Crown, ever since Parliament first attempted to exercise such control, centuries rather than decades ago.

Cash accounts, which simply record the payments and receipts of an organisation, are simple, quick and easy both to prepare and to understand. However, they provide a simplistic picture of what has happened in a year. Of course, they will show how much cash was spent, compared to plan, and how much cash was received, compared to plan. This does make it easy for Parliament, auditors and others to check that money was spent on the things for which it was intended and in the amounts that were intended.

Most people working within Government or close to Government are familiar with cash controls, such as cash limits and running cost controls. They are also familiar with annuality, essentially a consequence of cash control; if cash is not spent by 31 March it is lost, and cannot be carried forward and used in the following year, apart from some limited end-year flexibility. These controls can result in an enormous March spend, as the organisation tries to stay within, but only just within, the cash limit. This is increasingly recognised as a matter of good bookkeeping rather than of cash wisely spent.

The main problem of cash accounting is that it does not distinguish sufficiently between cash spent on running costs and cash invested for the future in capital items. Both are written off in the year they are spent. It is as though, after meeting your everyday living costs, you were to make no distinction between spending your salary on holidays, presents and gambling, as opposed to spending on a new car, clothes and furniture. True, at the end of the year all your cash may have gone in both cases, but in the second you have substantially more to carry forward to the next year. The cash actually paid out in a particular year, for example to buy a car, is unlikely to reflect the extent to which the resource is actually being used up or wearing out.

Cash accounting is concerned with reporting how cash was spent and received compared with what was authorised. Accruals accounting reports what was achieved and all the resources used in achieving those outputs, irrespective of when the cash was paid.

To those working in the public services, the requirement for public accountability is widely recognised and accepted. Many groups may be interested in the accounts of public sector organisations, for example (Henley et al 1993):

- Members of Parliament, councillors
- the public as voters or taxpayers
- customers, clients
- management, employees, unions
- competitors, suppliers
- Government - parent department, other departments, regulators
- financiers - H M Treasury, lenders, donors, sponsors, investors
- pressure groups.

These different groups will be interested in different information, and their needs will not always be compatible. Disclosure of information which would be in the interests of one group, say the public, might, for example, reveal too much to competitors. However, the view taken in recent times is that accruals accounting will generally improve accountability to all interested parties.

Improved accountability

The 1989 report on the financing and accountability of Next Steps Agencies gave the following reasons for the use of accruals accounting (HMSO 1989):

> These new accounts and reports will increase the transparency of Agencies' financial management and performance record to Parliament and its Committees and more widely. They will also support the Government's general drive towards improved financial management throughout the public services.

Similarly the 1993 *Financial Statement and Budget Report* (HM Treasury 1993) said:

> Resource accounting will help departments manage their finances and resources more effectively, and facilitate the further development of measures of departmental output and performance.

These key arguments are that accruals accounting effectively means:

- more openness
- improved financial management
- better measures of performance and financial control.

Ordnance Survey

Summary of outturn, and the Account of the sum expended, in the year ended 31 March 1993, compared with the sum granted, for expenditure by Ordnance Survey of Great Britain and other mapping services.

Summary of Outturn

Section	Estimated			Actual		
	Gross Expenditure	Appropriations in Aid	Net Expenditure	Gross Expenditure	Appropriations in Aid	Net Expenditure
	£000	£000	£000	£000	£000	£000
Records, Registrations and Surveys	£77,769	£55,854	£21,915	£77,676	£57,672	£20,004*

* This figure is £1,818,000 less than the net total of expenditure on the Appropriation Account, being the difference between the Appropriations in Aid realised (57,672,000) and those authorised to be applied (£55,854,000).

Account

Service	Grant	Expenditure	Expenditure compared with Grant	
			Less than Granted	More than Granted
Section A Records, Regulations and Surveys	£000	£000	£000	£000
A1 Running costs	63,800	63,763	37	–
A2 Superannuation	6,136	6,144	–	8
A3 Capital expenditure	4,818	4,755	63	–
A4 Payments to Customs and Excise	3,015	3,014	1	–

	£000			
Gross Total				
Original	79,417			
Supplementary	1,479			
Supplementary	(3,127)			
		77,769	77,676	101	8

	Estimated £000	Estimated £000		
Deduct				
AZ Appropriations in Aid				
Original	61,847			
Supplementary	(5,993)			
		55,854	55,854		

Net Total				
Original	17,570			
Supplementary	1,479			
Supplementary	2,866			
		21,915	21,822	Surplus 93 £92,771.80

Actual surplus to be surrendered

Figure 1.1 Appropriation account: Ordnance Survey.

❏ More openness

Are accruals accounts more transparent, more open, than cash accounts? The contrast between the cash accounts and the accruals accounts for Ordnance Survey shows how much more information accruals accounts present.

The cash accounts are shown in Figure 1.1. The accruals accounts, parts of which are shown in Chapters 5, 6 and 7, run in contrast to 16 pages.

Once organisations are more open about their financial performance, decisions can be made as a result. The early trading funds and candidates - Royal Dockyards, Royal Ordnance Factories and the Crown Suppliers - have all been privatised/contractorised/closed down. It is likely that their move to accruals accounts were useful in enabling others to see how well, or badly, they were performing.

Similar circumstances may have affected the re-privatised nationalised industries, such as British Airways, British Steel, British Telecom and British Gas. Some of the Executive Agencies, such as Vehicle Inspectorate, Patent Office and Companies House, also face privatisation after successful performance. Cash accounts would not have provided the information on the performance or the value of these organisations.

In the 1993 review of Next Steps, (CM 2430,1993), the conclusion was:

> The publication of agency Annual Reports and Accounts means that comprehensive information about the working of the Government machine is now readily available to anyone who wants it. This could previously have been obtained, if at all, only with considerable difficulty.

❏ Improved financial management

The key stages in improving financial management in the public sector, particularly central government, in recent years have been:

- Public Expenditure Survey   1960
- Fulton Report (accountable management)   1968
- cash limits   1976
- Efficiency Unit scrutinies   1979
- compulsory competitive tendering   1980 + 1988
- Financial Management Initiative (FMI)   1981
- National Audit Office value for money studies   1983
- privatisation   1983

- Next Steps   1987
- market testing   1992
- resource accounting   1994

Each of these has furthered progress towards better management of resources in government, towards better value for money. Next Steps and resource accounting are the two initiatives which have focused attention on and given a boost to accruals accounting.

❏ Improved measures of performance and financial control

With more financial information comes the ability to create better ways of setting targets and measuring financial performance. Many of these are discussed in detail in Chapter 10, and include breakeven, cost recovery and return on assets. The Next Steps Review (Cm2430,1993) stated that:

> Financial control has been strengthened, and all agencies have clear financial targets.

❏ Business-like approach

The advantage of accruals accounting is that it allows an organisation to be run in a more business-like way. Herbert Morrison (1942) argued that:

> An enterprise does not have to be private in order to be enterprise.

Similarly, an organisation does not have to be private in order to be managed in a business-like way. Accruals accounting has traditionally been associated with private business and a business approach to financial reporting and financial management. The Next Steps Review (1993) stated:

> Regardless of whether or not they can trade, agencies are required to publish commercial-style accounts, on an accruals basis. If they are not able to do so when they launch, the aim is that such accounts should be produced within two years of launch. This is encouraging a more business-like approach and providing harder information from which agencies can work to improve efficiency.

It is useful to refer to two other developments which support this view.

First, the governments of New Zealand and New South Wales already produce accruals accounts, and Australia, USA, Canada, Iceland and Eire are all moving the same way. An OECD report in 1993 shows how the public sector in other parts of the world also considers it helpful to report in this more business–like way.

Secondly, a Treasury report over 160 years ago, on departmental accounts

(HM Treasury 1829), proposed that:

> an abstract of the expenditure, with a Balance Sheet, might, at the close of each month, year, or any given period, be easily prepared... We have offered these suggestions in the fullest persuasion that they are calculated essentially to promote objects of the highest interest and importance - the eventual attainment of a complete simplification of the Accounts, and a perfectly economical arrangement of the Public Business.

If it has taken since 1829, and the process is still not complete, perhaps this book may help us to take a few more steps down the road of understanding and change. It should explain the reasons for the enthusiasm for accruals accounting in the various quotations in this chapter.

References

Cm 2430
Next Steps Agencies in Government Review 1993
HMSO, London   1993

Cm 914
The Financing and Accountability of Next Steps Agencies
HMSO, London   1989

Henley, Likierman, Perrin, Evans, Lapsley and Whiteoak
Public Sector Accounting and Financial Control (4th ed)
Chapman and Hall, London   1993

H Morrison
As reported in Observer Sayings of the Week
                                                    27 December 1942.

Organisation for Economic Co-operation and Development
Accounting for what?: the value of accrual accounting to the public sector
OECD, Paris   1993

H M Treasury
Report of the Commissioners appointed to inquire into and state the mode of keeping the official accounts in the principal departments connected with the receipts and expenditure for the public service
Unpublished   1829

Chapter 2

Where accruals accounts exist

The diversity of the programmes of government enterprise, the differences in their forms of organization, and the prescribed financial control requirements impose a variety of reporting needs. In all cases, there are basic requirements for a balance sheet, profit and loss statements and statements of the source and application of funds (United Nations, 1970)

Accruals accounts exist in a number of areas of the public sector. By way of background, this chapter briefly describes these areas, which are:

- the national accounts
- Government departments
- non-departmental public bodies (NDPBs)
- nationalised industries
- public corporations
- the National Health Service
- local authorities
- charities
- educational institutions
- housing associations.

National accounts

The national accounts measure the activity of the whole UK economy, in all sectors. The national accounts are prepared by the Central Statistical Office and conform with an internationally agreed framework. They are built up from separate accounts for each sector, and combine production accounts, income and expenditure accounts, capital accounts and financial accounts. All are prepared on the accruals basis. These accounts can be used to calculate gross domestic product (GDP) and gross national product (GNP), as well as other measures of the economy. The national accounts are not discussed further in this book.

Government Departments

There are 50 Government departments, spending some £ 173bn and with 550,000 staff.

They range from the very large, the Department of Social Security, with a (cash) spend in 1994-95 of £75bn, and 91,000 staff, to the smallest, the Northern Ireland Office, with 200 staff. There are also non-ministerial departments, such as the utility regulators OFGAS, OFWAT, OFTEL and OFFER.

At present, the funding for these departments is provided and controlled on a cash basis, on cash actually paid and actually received. The planning and control system has three elements:

- the Public Expenditure Survey, which looks 3 years ahead and plans payments and receipts, but provides no formal authorisation for the expenditure
- the supply estimates (vote funding) which are voted by Parliament and provide the formal approval for the expenditure of cash for one year ahead
- the Appropriation accounts, which report what was actually spent and received in cash compared to the estimate approved by Parliament.

The problem with this system was recognised by the Chancellor of the Exchequer (Clarke 1993):

> Government accounting for public spending has become archaic. In my view, the time has come to move to a system of accounting which identifies more clearly the cost of resources. This will put departments onto a similar accounting basis to commercial organisations and many other parts of the public sector.

The exact scope and format of these 'resource accounts' are under development, and they will be introduced over three to five years. It is likely that they will adopt most of the principles of accruals accounting. However, while the main planning and control system is currently based almost exclusively on cash, there are some areas where accruals accounts are already in use.

❑ Fees and charges operations

A fees and charges operation exists wherever a fee or charge is levied for services or goods supplied, either within government departments or to the public. There are a few hundred such operations where annual costs exceed £1m, and many hundreds more below that limit. The largest fees and charges operations have become Executive Agencies.

The remainder have been required since 1983 to produce accruals based accounts, known as memorandum trading accounts, following the *Fees and Charges Guide*. These are prepared to show that the charges raised are a fair reflection of all costs incurred, not just the cash paid out in a particular year.

❑ Executive Agencies

As at 30 April 1994 there were 97 Executive Agencies. These have been set up since 1988 under the Next Steps initiative, a programme designed to use available resources to deliver better quality central Government services, for the benefit of taxpayers, customers and staff. The Agencies range from the smallest, Wilton Park Conference Centre (part of the FCO) with 25 staff, to Social Security Benefits Agency, with 64,000. Including Customs and Excise and Inland Revenue, which operate on Next Steps lines, Agencies cover 348,000 staff in total, about 60% of the civil service.

Twelve of these Agencies have become trading funds (see below). The rest, the majority, receive some or all of their finance as vote funding, subject to the same rules as the rest of government. However, besides producing cash accounts, they also have to produce accruals accounts. For a few Agencies, such as Ordnance Survey, this did not involve a change, but the majority have had to make the transition.

❑ Trading funds

A trading fund is a financial regime under which the organisation, which may be an Executive Agency which is a complete Government department, or an Executive Agency within a department, is freed from the vote accounting system and instead is required to:

- produce full commercial accounts
- break even taking one year with another and
- to meet a particular financial target.

The trading funds at 30 April 94 were:

Departments and Executive Agencies:
- The Royal Mint
- Her Majesty's Stationery Office
- Central Office of Information

Executive Agencies:
- Companies House
- Vehicle Inspectorate

- Patent Office
- Fire Service College
- Land Registry
- Chessington Computer Centre
- The Buying Agency
- Medicines Control Agency
- Defence Research Agency.

Trading funds need to receive at least 51% of their funds from arms-length operations. They may receive subsidies from votes if necessary, though the majority do not. Any extra cash needed for capital can be borrowed, subject to interest and repayment, from their parent department if there is one, otherwise from the National Loans Fund, but this is controlled as an External Finance Limit in the Public Expenditure Survey.

Trading funds have greater freedom to manage their own cash. The traditional cash rules of annuality and running cost controls do not apply. They can invest surplus cash and earn interest.

The legislation for trading funds is the Government Trading Funds Act 1973, as amended by the Government Trading Act 1990 and subsequent Finance Acts. The original legislation restricted trading fund status to organisations who were trading, effectively in competition with the private sector, while the 1990 Act widened the scope to include an organisation whose income consists 'principally of receipts in respect of goods and services', even if it is a statutory monopoly.

❏ Commercial operations

There are a few organisations in central government which have been operating commercially and were preparing accruals accounts before Next Steps was launched. They are not and may never become Executive Agencies. These are:

- The Crown Estate, which is not the property of the Government but managed by a statutory corporation, the Crown Estate Commissioners, and its surplus rents and profits are surrendered to Parliament.
- Export Credit Guarantee Department – a Government department
- Forestry Commission – a Government department

Non-departmental public bodies

Non–departmental public bodies are sometimes referred to as QUANGOs (quasi-autonomous non-governmental organisations). NDPBs receive some or all of their funding from a government department, but are not a department, and operate to a greater or lesser degree at arm's-length from Ministers.

The Cabinet Office guide, *Public Bodies 1993* lists 1,389 NDPBs at 1 April 1993. They are classified as:

- **executive bodies,** which carry out prescribed functions within government guidelines. There were 358 of these, and examples are Royal Botanic Gardens, Kew, Remploy Limited, English Nature, Highlands and Islands Enterprise, Monopolies and Mergers Commission and Northern Lighthouse Board. The total spent is about £15bn

- **advisory bodies,** which are set up to advise Ministers and their departments. These NDPBs do not usually employ staff or incur expenditure on their own account. There were 829 of these, ranging from the Royal Fine Art Commission through the Expert Advisory Group on AIDS to the Government Hospitality Fund Advisory Committee for the Purchase of Wine

- **tribunals,** of which there were 68, including the Social Security Appeal Tribunals

- **134 other bodies,** mainly prison visitor boards.

Not all bodies fit neatly into a single category. For example, English Nature has both executive and advisory functions. Some executive NDPBs such as Scottish Homes and the United Kingdom Atomic Energy Authority are classified as public corporations for public expenditure control and national accounts purposes.

Executive NDPBs have been required for some years to prepare accruals accounts. Some operate fees and charges operations, in which case the *Fees and Charges Guide* applies. The speed of the change from cash to accruals accounts seems to depend on the sponsoring department, the size of the NDPB and the enthusiasm of the NDPB.

Nationalised industries

Nationalised industries are publicly owned bodies, usually set up under their own statutes, and run by boards appointed by ministers. Many are monopolies, and their continued existence in the public sector is a legacy of the drive to nationalisation of the immediate post-war years. Over the past 15 years the number of nationalised industries has decreased, as they have been progressively privatised (although the actual number will increase slightly as new organisations are incorporated to facilitate the restructuring of the rail industry).

Those at present and their sponsoring departments are:

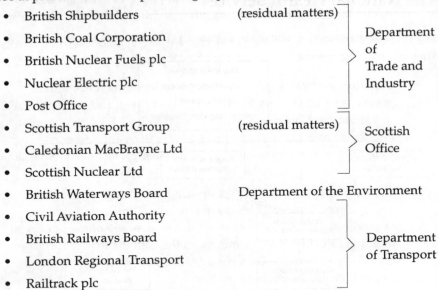

- British Shipbuilders (residual matters)
- British Coal Corporation
- British Nuclear Fuels plc
- Nuclear Electric plc
- Post Office

Department of Trade and Industry

- Scottish Transport Group (residual matters)
- Caledonian MacBrayne Ltd
- Scottish Nuclear Ltd

Scottish Office

- British Waterways Board — Department of the Environment

- Civil Aviation Authority
- British Railways Board
- London Regional Transport
- Railtrack plc

Department of Transport

These all produce accruals accounts.

❏ Public corporations

These are similar to nationalised industries, except that they are not actually industries. They are:

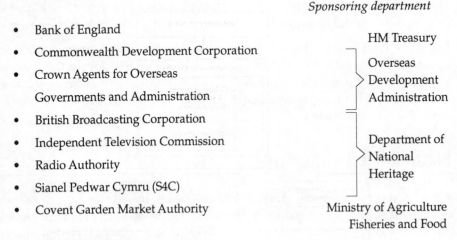

Sponsoring department

- Bank of England

HM Treasury

- Commonwealth Development Corporation
- Crown Agents for Overseas
  Governments and Administration

Overseas Development Administration

- British Broadcasting Corporation
- Independent Television Commission
- Radio Authority
- Sianel Pedwar Cymru (S4C)

Department of National Heritage

- Covent Garden Market Authority

Ministry of Agriculture Fisheries and Food

These also produce accruals accounts.

The National Health Service

The NHS is structured as shown in Figure 2.1 (Henley et al 1993):

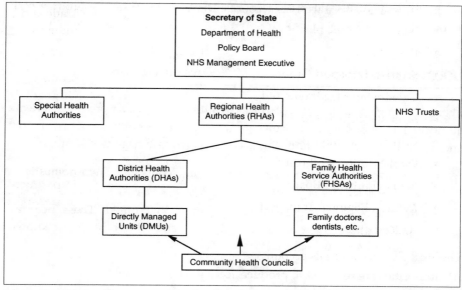

Figure 2.1 NHS organisation structure in England.

The Regional Health Authorities will be abolished in 1996, and the new organisational arrangement will be as shown in Figure 2.2.

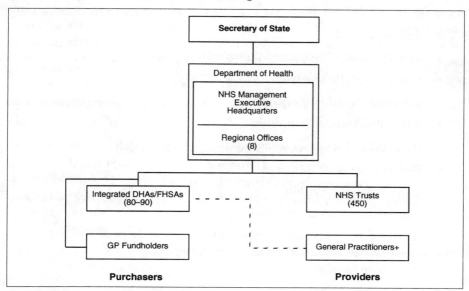

Figure 2.2 New structure of the NHS.

The bulk of NHS funds come from the Department of Health with 4% from charges and 1% from capital receipts. NHS Trusts receive all their funding by selling their services to other parts of the NHS, so they are similar to trading funds. The District Health Authorities, Family Health Service Authorities, NHS Trusts and GP fundholders all produce accruals accounts. DHAs and FHSAs also produce cash accounts.

Local authorities

There is a range of different types of local authority areas. At present, there are authorities for London, and elsewhere there are metropolitan, county, district and, in Scotland, regional authorities. They receive cash from two sources:

- the cash which they collect locally through council tax, non-domestic rates and fees for services
- the grants which they receive from central Government. These include specific grants, such as that for the Police, and the general grant, known as revenue support grant.

All authorities are required to produce accruals style accounts.

Charities

A charity can be defined as a body whose income is applied to charitable purposes, which are the relief of poverty, the advancement of education, the advancement of religion or other purposes beneficial to the community. Although charities might be thought to belong in the voluntary sector, rather than the public sector, there are some which receive public funds.

These include many of the charities which are classified as exempt charities in the Charities Act 1993, which include:

- the universities of Oxford, Cambridge, London, Durham and Newcastle, the colleges and halls in the universities of Oxford, Cambridge, Durham and Newcastle, Queen Mary and Westfield College in the University of London and the colleges of Winchester and Eton
- any university, university college, or institution connected with a university or university college, which Her Majesty declares by Order in Council to be an exempt charity for the purposes of this Act
- a grant-maintained school

- the National Curriculum Council
- the Curriculum Council for Wales
- the School Examinations and Assessment Council
- the Board of Trustees of the Victoria and Albert Museum
- the Board of Trustees of the Science Museum
- the Board of Trustees of the Armouries
- the Board of Trustees of the Royal Botanic Gardens, Kew
- the British Library Board.

Other public sector charities include the British Council, which is the largest British charity, and the Arts Council.

Exempt charities are required to produce accruals accounts. The requirements for all other charities are under review and being developed, and it is very likely that larger charities will also have to produce accruals accounts.

Educational institutions

The main groups in this sector are:

- Universities
- Further education institutions
- Grant maintained schools and city technology colleges
- Local Education Authority (LEA) schools.

Universities include both the 'old' universities, such as Oxford and Manchester, and the 'new' universities, the former polytechnics and colleges, such as Oxford Brookes and Manchester Metropolitan. All are recommended to produce accruals accounts by the Committee of Vice-Chancellors and Principals. Further education institutions, including sixth form colleges, are required to prepare accruals accounts, as are grant maintained schools and city technology colleges.

LEA schools who have delegated budgets under the local management of schools (LMS) produce limited cash information for their local authority. This gets assimilated in the local authority's own accounts.

Housing associations

A housing association is a non-profit making body providing housing for those in need. There are some 2,300 registered associations in England, of which 600 receive grants totalling £2.4bn for capital developments. They are regulated by the Housing Corporation, an executive NDPB of the Department of the Environment.

The associations are private sector bodies, but as they receive a significant amount of public money, they have been included in the scope of this book. They may be set up as charities, or as friendly societies, and are required to produce accruals accounts.

References

Cabinet Office
Public Bodies 1993
HMSO, London   1993

Cabinet Office and H M Treasury
Non-departmental public bodies : a guide for departments
Cabinet Office and HM Treasury, London   1992

Kenneth Clarke
Budget Speech 30.11.1993
As reported in Hansard Col 931
HMSO, London   1993

United Nations
A manual for government accounting
Geneva   1970

Chapter 3

Principles of accruals accounting

Write about money, and you cannot entirely avoid technical terms (Brett, 1987)

Various terms are used to mean the same, or very similar, forms of accounting. These are:

- accruals accounting
- commercial accounting
- business accounting
- financial accounting.

Throughout this book, the term accruals accounting will be used, even though in some circumstances organisations may apply some, but not all, of the principles.

Cash and accruals accounting contrasted

To understand the principles of accruals accounting, it is useful to start by comparing them with the principles of cash accounting.

❏ Cash accounting

Under cash accounting, income is recognised at the point in time when money is received by an organisation, and costs are recognised at the point in time when payment is made. All the receipts and payments (and only those receipts and payments) made in a specified period will be included in the cash accounts for that period, irrespective of the period of activity to which the costs or income actually relate. So, for example, cash spent on the last day of the year to fill up a tank of heating oil will be treated as a cost, even though the oil will not be used until after the end of the year.

For a Government department, the Appropriation account is a cash accounting summary, showing what was actually spent and received in a year compared to what was authorised in the Supply Estimate. The Appropriation account for Ordnance Survey was shown in Chapter 1 as an example of this type of accounting.

No distinction is made between cash which is paid out for capital expenditure (e.g. buying a building) and that which is current expenditure (e.g. staff costs). At the end of the period cash accounting usually shows only the value of bank and cash balances. Cash accounting does not permit the construction of a balance sheet, a statement showing the net worth of the organisation.

Cash accounting provides a simple and effective method of reporting the total amount spent by an organisation, and is essential if control of the total cash is what is required. However, it does not reflect everything that has happened in the organisation, particularly as far as the consumption of resources is concerned, and will not provide a way of measuring the organisation's overall performance. For example it does not include the cost of using items, such as buildings, where the cash was paid in a previous period.

❑ Accruals accounting

Under accruals accounting, rather than looking at receipts and payments, income is recognised when it is earned and costs are recognised when they are incurred (when the resources are consumed). The actual timing of the receipt or payment of cash is irrelevant.

Income is earned when the services or goods are provided to the customer, and may include items where the cash was received in an earlier period, or is to be collected in a later period. Costs are incurred when the goods and services are received or used, and may not yet have been paid, or indeed may have been paid some years before, where the resource (e.g. equipment) is still being used. Accruals accounting allows the income earned from services or goods to be properly matched with the costs incurred in delivering the services or providing the goods.

The statement showing what has happened in accruals terms over the period is the operating account. The value of everything the organisation still owns and owes at the end of the period is shown in a balance sheet. These are the two key statements that result from the use of accruals accounting.

Fundamental accounting concepts

Underpinning accruals accounting are a number of concepts. The first four of these, the fundamental accounting concepts, originated in private sector accounting, and were first set out in Statement of Standard Accounting Practice 2 (SSAP2) in 1971. (The Statements of Standard Accounting Practice are discussed in detail in Chapter 8.) They were then embodied in the Companies Act 1981, and currently are contained in Sch 4 of the Companies Act 1985.

SSAP2 states:

Fundamental accounting concepts are the broad basic assumptions which underlie the periodic financial accounts of business enterprises.

At the present time the four following fundamental concepts (the relative importance of which will vary according to the circumstances of the particular case) are regarded as having general acceptability:

a) the 'going concern' concept: the enterprise will continue in operational existence for the foreseeable future. This means in particular that the profit and loss account and balance sheet assume no intention or necessity to liquidate or curtail significantly the scale of operation;

b) the 'accruals' concept: revenue and costs are accrued (that is, recognised as they are earned or incurred, not as money is received or paid), matched with one another so far as their relationship can be established or justifiably assumed, and dealt with in the profit and loss account of the period to which they relate; provided that where the accruals concept is inconsistent with the 'prudence' concept (paragraph [d] below), the latter prevails. The accruals concept implies that the profit and loss account reflects changes in the amount of net assets that arise out of the transactions of the relevant period (other than distributions or subscriptions of capital and unrealised surpluses arising on revaluation of fixed assets). Revenue and profits dealt with in the profit and loss account are matched with associated costs and expenses by including in the same account the costs incurred in earning them (so far as these are material and identifiable);

c) the 'consistency' concept: there is consistency of accounting treatment of like items within each accounting period and from one period to the next;

d) the concept of 'prudence': revenue and profits are not anticipated, but are recognised by inclusion in the profit and loss account only when realised in the form either of cash or of other assets the ultimate cash realisation of which can be assessed with reasonable certainty; provision is made for all known liabilities (expenses and losses) whether the amount of these is known with certainty or is a best estimate in the light of the information available.

Each of these concepts is considered to be so fundamental that they are all assumed to be followed in the preparation of a set of accruals accounts, and no mention will be made of them anywhere in the accounts unless there is a particular problem in applying one or more of them.

The significance of each of the concepts may be more easily understood by considering what difference it would make to the accounts if an organisation chose not to apply one, in part or all of the accounts.

❑ Going concern

The going concern concept means that the valuation of items in the accounts is only the value to that same organisation carrying on in roughly the same way. If an organisation were not valued as a going concern, then it might be valued on one of two other bases, break-up value or sale value.

If the intention were to dispose of the organisation piece-meal, then on a break-up valuation the value of the organisation would probably be much less. The sum of the parts would be less than the whole. Each item would be subject to scrutiny by those buying, and they might be prepared to pay much less for the stock than it was worth to the current owners. In addition, there might be additional costs, such as redundancy, to be included if the organisation were broken up.

If the valuation was on the basis of a sale to a willing buyer, it might be much more than a going concern value, as a potential buyer would value items such as the customers and likely future income streams, neither of which will have been included in the going concern accounts.

❑ Relevance of going concern concept to public sector organisations

It is somewhat problematical to apply this assumption automatically to organisations in the public sector. They have much less control over their own continued existence than a private sector business, where the directors and shareholders control the future to a much greater degree. Sometimes public sector organisations might be thought to depend on political whim for their survival, and many depend on an annual vote of Parliament to provide their funding. It is notable that, in two guidance documents on accruals accounts, H M Treasury (1988 and 1993) omits the going concern assumption, while including all the others from SSAP2 in its requirements. The CIPFA *Code of Practice on Local Authority Accounting* (1993) also omits this concept.

This might be because, as claimed by Henley et al (1993):

> The vast majority of public sector organisations cannot 'go broke'. Except in very special circumstances the government would be expected to step in to support the public sector.

In practice, though, public sector organisations will have to assume that they are a going concern in preparing their accounts, as reasonable assumptions such as the expected life of capital items could not otherwise be made. Only where there is a definite likelihood of the organisation's not continuing need there be reference to it in the accounts, and a change in the valuation method.

❏ Accruals

This concept is also referred to as the matching concept, in that income and the costs incurred in earning that income are matched to the relevant period.

There are two main alternatives to the accruals basis in drawing up accounts. One is the cash basis, mentioned above, where receipts and payments are included as they occur.

The other, less common, method is commitment accounting. This recognises cost much earlier than accruals accounting. As soon as the organisation places an order for goods or services, it recognises the cost and the fact that it owes the money for those goods or services. Commitment accounting is a very effective way of controlling costs, particularly where costs have to be kept within fixed budgets. It is a powerful form of management accounting, but it recognises the cost too early for accruals. Accruals accounting waits until the goods or services have been received.

❏ Consistency

If an organisation were not consistent in the ways it applied its approach to its accounting, between items and between years, it might choose to change assumptions in the accounts to present a distorted or more favourable picture. For example, a £10,000 vehicle expected to last 4 years and to have no scrap value, would be charged at £2,500 a year. If this is changed to charging over 6 years to reduce the costs to £1,667 a year, or to over 3 years to increase costs to £3,333, and the vehicle will in fact still last 4 years, then the treatment is not being consistent and the accounts are misleading. If a second identical vehicle is charged over 5 years at £2,000, then again the figures are being distorted.

Clearly, where reality has changed and it has been realised that the vehicle will actually have a longer or shorter life, then this should be reflected in the way the accounts are prepared. The accounts should never be allowed to be consistently wrong by continuing to charge for the vehicle over 4 years.

❏ Prudence

Part of the impact of using accruals accounting is that certain items are included before their outcome is certain in cash terms. For example, sales are recognised when the income is earned, before the cash is received. If gains were anticipated, i.e. recognised before they were certain, then there would be a risk that the gain might never materialise and the accounts would be overstated. Chickens cannot be counted before they hatch. An example would be where an organisation included any stock items at their potential sale value, rather than following prudence which is to value at the lower of cost and net realisable value (sale proceeds less costs to be incurred in selling). The prudence principle allows the gain made on selling the stock to fall into the period in which the stock is actually sold.

Similarly, if probable losses were not included, then the accounts might again be overstated. If the organisation is owed money by customers, and it is known that one of those customers is likely not to be able to pay up in full, then prudence would indicate that only the amount likely to be recovered should be included.

It may result from the application of prudence that the accounts are understated, both as to the value of items and as to the amount of gains included. It is considered that this is preferable to overstating the results. SSAP2 specifically states that prudence overrides accruals.

Other concepts

There are two other concepts which, though not included in SSAP2, are essential to an understanding of accruals accounts. They are materiality and substance over form.

❑ Materiality

Cash accounts can be accurate, as they record what has actually taken place, and the bank balance and cash at the end of the period can be checked against actual amounts held. Accruals accounts cannot be regarded as accurate or correct in the same sense, because of the way in which they are prepared. Many of the items in accruals accounts have to be estimated, such as how much should be charged for the use of a vehicle. In reality the vehicle will never last exactly the predicted time with exactly the predicted scrap value, and the charge each year will be too high or too low.

Because of the estimates involved, accruals accounts are only required to give a 'true and fair' view, or to 'present fairly' the results. The Companies Act 1947 introduced the term 'true and fair'. True and fair is not defined in the Act, but can be taken to mean that the accounts will not mislead a reasonable user. This does mean that, when preparing accounts, an organisation can include reasonable estimates and does not need to wait to see the final outcome. The effect of this concept on the audit of accruals accounts is covered in Chapter 9.

❑ Substance over form

The term 'substance over form' is shorthand for 'accounting substance over legal form'. This concept means that the accounts should reflect the underlying commercial nature of a transaction, rather than being constrained by the legal status. A common example is lease purchase of equipment. Under the lease, the equipment does not legally become the property of the buying organisation until the final payment is made. In reality, what is happening is that the buying organisation is using the lease as a form of interest bearing loan with which to buy the equipment. Substance over form will ensure that the equipment appears in the accounts as being owned by the organisation from the start of the lease period, with the corresponding amount owed to the lessor also shown.

References

Accounting Standards Committee
Statement of Standard Accounting Practice 2
ICAEW, London   1971

Brett
How to read the financial pages
Century Hutchinson, London   1987

Chartered Institute of Public Finance and Accountancy
Code of Practice on Local Authority Accounting
CIPFA, London   1993

Henley, Likierman, Perrin, Evans, Lapsley and Whiteoak
Public Sector Accounting and Financial Control (4th Ed)
Chapman & Hall, London   1993

H M Treasury
Central Government : Financial Accounting and Reporting Framework
HMSO, London   1988

H M Treasury
Next Steps Agencies : Annual Reports and Accounts
Unpublished   1993

Chapter 4

Cost

The concept of cost cannot be very specific. It all depends upon what one means by cost. (Walker 1982)

This topic is included because it is important to understand that there are different ways in which a cost figure may be reached. The same source information can be analysed in a number of ways to arrive at different figures for cost. The different methods used have a significant effect on the results presented in the accounts.

There are several different ways of looking at costs which in themselves have no significance in the production of statutory accruals accounts. Examples are:

- fixed costs and variable costs
- controllable and non-controllable costs
- direct and indirect costs
- marginal costs
- sunk costs
- opportunity costs
- incremental costs
- life cycle costs.

While not significant for accruals accounts the above ways of considering costs *will* play an important part in management accounting and decision making.

Historical or current costs

Accruals costs are those costs incurred in earning the income for the period. They will include staff costs, accommodation costs and charges for the use of capital items. Some of these costs will have been paid in cash in the period in question, others may have been paid before or after that period. The first choice that has to be made is between the historical cost and the current cost basis of determining the cost. This will have a significant effect on the charge for capital items and the value of assets shown in the balance sheet.

❏ Historical cost

This is the actual price paid, either for a capital item or an expense. For example, an organisation bought a building for £29,000 in 1932, or the organisation bought £5,000 of stationery in the period.

The advantages of using historical cost in the accounts are that it is:

- simple, as once a transaction has been recorded then the amount at which it is recorded does not change
- easily understood by ordinary readers of the accounts
- relatively objective and reliable
- difficult to manipulate
- more popular with the managers of the organisation, as, in times of rising prices, it will usually reduce the reported costs, and hence increase the reported surplus.

The disadvantages of using historical cost are:

- the accounts will contain information which may be very out of date, and may not provide a picture of the current state of the organisation
- the organisation may not realise the extent to which its apparently successful performance and growth are due simply to rising price
- the organisation may distribute or surrender some of the apparent surplus disclosed under historical cost, which in fact should be retained within the organisation
- it may fail to bid for the total resources it requires to deliver a service, or fail to set charges at a high enough level to recover all the costs.

In summary, this basis will fail to prepare accounts which show whether the organisation has managed to maintain its operating capacity.

❏ Modified historical cost

This method recognises that land and buildings in particular, but also other tangible items, do change in value over time. This change in value is brought into the accounts by revaluation of the items concerned. As a result of the change in value, there will also be a change in the charge made for the use of that item.

In private sector accounts, this revaluation is usually carried out at intervals to suit the managers of the business, usually only when the movements in the property market have been favourable and significant. The guidance followed in the public sector is that revaluation of all capital items should be carried out every year.

The approach to the valuation may differ according to whether it is necessary to value:

- land and buildings
- equipment
- stock.

Land and buildings

The revaluation of land and buildings can most cost-effectively be achieved not by valuing every item of property every year, but by taking, say, a representative one third of the portfolio and getting it valued professionally. The following year a different third of the property would be inspected and valued.

Valuation could be carried out by the District Valuer, the Valuation Office of the Inland Revenue, by the Property Services Agency or by private firms. If the organisation had sufficiently skilled internal valuers, then their valuation might be used, although it would probably be considered by auditors to be subject to bias and less independent than that of an external valuer.

The resultant percentage change (increase or decrease) in value since the last valuation of the property inspected could then be applied to all the rest of the property held.

Alternatively, a property price index, such as that included in the Valuation Office *Property Market Report*, published every 6 months, may provide a close enough approximation to the actual price movement on property for the organisation.

Equipment

Equipment, computers and other capital items may be more cost effectively valued by looking at the movement in the appropriate price index, rather than by considering individual items. This approach is more suitable because of the relatively short life of equipment compared to property. The organisation may be able to generate sufficient information to create its own indices. The Central Statistical Office publishes a monthly Business Monitor series. Monthly Monitor number 17 (MM17) provides price index numbers for current cost accounting, and Monthly Monitor number 22 (MM22) provides producer price indices, which cover a variety of items, and may give a better spread.

By revaluing the capital items in the accounts, the balance sheet will usually show over a number of years a higher value than the historical cost balance sheet. Similarly, the cost of consuming those resources will increase.

Stock

The modified historical cost approach is also applied to stock, provided that there is a significant amount of stock held for a significant time. The stock is valued at replacement cost in the balance sheet, and the cost of stock consumed in the period is increased to the cost of replacing that stock at the price it would cost at the end of the period.

The advantages of modified historical cost are:

- it charges to the accounts a cost based on the real value of items consumed
- it shows the real value of the organisation in today's money
- it should ensure that charges set to customers can be shown to collect enough to replace the items used in providing the services or goods, at the price they will cost when the time comes to replace them.

The disadvantages are:

- it is more complicated
- it is time consuming
- it produces 'hypothetical' figures which move away from the price that was known to have been paid
- there is a problem when valuations show a fall in value of items held - see the accounts of Ordnance Survey in Chapter 6
- organisations using this method may seem to be at a disadvantage when they are operating in competition with private sector organisations who, on the whole, use historical cost. This may not be a real disadvantage, as such private sector organisations can only ignore the effect of inflation in their pricing policies for a short time. In reality, most will have to build inflation assumptions into their pricing even if not into their external reporting.

❑ Current cost

This takes the modified historical cost method, and adds more adjustments to costs. It follows the approach of SSAP 16, which was in force until 1985. Although SSAP 16 is now withdrawn, the guidance in *Accounting for the effects of changing prices: a Handbook*, (Accounting Standards Committee, 1986) follows the same approach.

The adjustments made to historical cost are, firstly, the same as those in the modified historical cost approach, namely:

- revaluation of capital items, and charges on that basis
- increase in the cost of stock and hence cost of sales.

There are two further adjustments, the monetary working capital adjustment and the gearing adjustment.

Monetary working capital adjustment

This takes into account the effect of rising prices on two other parts of the balance sheet. In so far as an organisation's customers receive credit, and take some time to pay, then, when prices are rising, the value of the cash received in a few weeks' or months' time is less than if it were received at once. Similarly, if the organisation takes some time to pay its suppliers, then in times of inflation the amount to be paid does not rise, so the effective cost is less.

The monetary working capital adjustment (MWCA) looks at the net amount owed to the organisation by its customers and by the organisation to its suppliers, and adjusts for the change in value caused by the net delay in paying or receiving cash. This is shown in Figure 4.1.

An organisation is owed £100,000 by customers, and owes £40,000 to suppliers. The net amount of monetary working capital is £60,000. If prices rise at 10% over the year, and at the end of the year monetary working capital is £80,000, then the MWCA is calculated as:

a) **Total increase** = £80,000 − £60,000 = £20,000

b) **Volume increase** = closing figure x $\dfrac{\text{average index}}{\text{closing index}}$ - opening figure x $\dfrac{\text{average index}}{\text{opening index}}$

$$= \left[£80,000 \times \frac{105}{110} \right] - \left[£60,000 \times \frac{105}{100} \right]$$

$$= £76,364 - £63,000 = £13,364$$

c) **MWCA** = total increase − volume increase

$$= a) - b)$$

$$= £20,000 - £13,364 = £6,636$$

Figure 4.1 Calculating the MWCA.

The adjustment can be to the organisation's advantage if it collects from its customers faster than it pays its suppliers.

Gearing adjustment

The gearing adjustment only applies to organisations which are funded by two different types of finance, loans and shareholders' funds. It reflects the fact that, in times of rising prices, loan funding remains a fixed amount, and requires a fixed return, whereas shareholders' funds need increasing reward.

If an organisation is funded by £750,000 from shareholders and £250,000 from loans, then the proportion of the total funding which is from loans is 25%. This is used to calculate the proportionate reduction in the three costs above - depreciation, cost of sales and monetary working capital. If those three costs totalled £40,000, the gearing adjustment would be £10,000.

As most public sector organisations usually rely completely on the Exchequer and the taxpayer for their funding, this adjustment does not arise. It does appear in the accounts of those private sector organisations, such as British Gas, who still prepare current cost accounts.

❏ Where is current cost accounting used?

Nationalised industries have prepared current cost accounts under SSAP16 for a number of years. The Byatt Report (1986) reviewed the situation and concluded that:

> Current Cost Accounting (CCA) is particularly important in nationalised industries, because of the long life of their assets and because their economic performance has to be assessed in the absence of fully competitive markets.

> The CCA principle of valuing assets at their current value to the business is the right basis for measuring continuing capital costs.

As a result, the annual accounts drawn up by each nationalised industry are expected to reflect the effect of changing prices. Industries vary in the extent to which they adopt current cost principles; some produce comprehensive CCA accounts as a supplement to their historical cost accounts (e.g. Civil Aviation Authority); others produce only one set of modified historical cost accounts (e.g. London Transport, Post Office); whilst some publish only additional current cost information on certain categories of assets (e.g. British Coal.)

There are two remaining trading funds of those set up while SSAP 16 was in force, the Royal Mint set up in 1975 and Her Majesty's Stationery Office set up in 1980. They are still required to produce current cost accounts, as well as historic cost accounts with revalued property. Their financial targets (see Chapter 10) are set in current cost terms.

It is interesting to note that British Telecom changed its method of accounting from current cost to historical cost after privatisation.

❑ Choice of cost method

If the choice seems confusing to the non-expert, it may help to consider that, during the accounting profession's years of developing the (now abandoned) approach to inflation accounting, Douglas Morpeth, chairman of one of the Inflation Accounting Steering Groups, said:

> Which would you rather have, accounts which are precisely wrong, or accounts which are approximately correct?

In the private sector, the choice is left open to companies. The Companies Act 1985, Sch 4, states that companies should either use historical cost as set out in Section B of the Act or current cost or modified historical cost as set out in Section C.

In the public sector, historical cost is not an option, and the choice is only between current cost and modified historical cost. Because there is a choice, all organisations must always disclose in their accounts which method they have used, so that a user of the accounts can understand the context of the figures.

❑ Notional costs

These are costs where, although the cost is incurred by the organisation, it may actually be borne by another part of the public sector, or fall at a very remote time.

Examples of notional costs are:

- insurance
- interest on capital
- free services.

Insurance

Most public sector organisations do not take out commercial insurance cover for risks such as fire, theft, other loss of property, employers' liability or public liability. The reason for not insuring commercially is that the public sector is such a large organisation that the annual cost of claims is less than the premiums which would need to be paid to the commercial insurance companies to cover the claims, their administrative costs and profits.

The effect of this on an individual organisation means that some years there will be small claims, and in other years higher claims. This can be seen in Figure 4.2.

In practice, it would be difficult to justify charging, say, £10 more for a passport or a hip replacement operation in the year that a large claim fell. Across the whole of the public sector the peaks and troughs will roughly even out, so there is a constant level of claim on the Exchequer. To smooth out these peaks and troughs in the individual organisation, a notional charge is made for insurance, following rates based on the experience of the organisation, or rates issued by HM Treasury. This is shown in Figure 4.3.

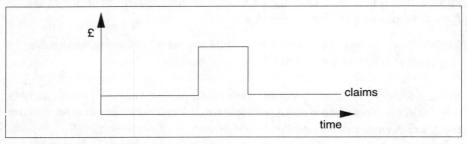

Figure 4.2. Cash costs of uninsured claims.

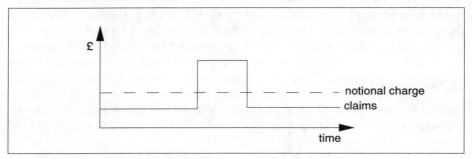

Figure 4.3. Cash costs and notional charges of uninsured claims.

This has the effect that in most years more will be charged by way of notional premiums than is paid out in cash, so extra cash is collected from the organisation's customers. This will effectively be surrendered back to the Treasury as excess receipts. In the year where the large claim arises, the organisation can try to meet the cost out of its own resources. If it fails it can go to Treasury and ask for cash to make good the claim. Chapter 27 of *Government Accounting* has more information on insurance.

Interest on capital

This is a notional cost only for those organisations where it is not an actual cost. Trading funds, NHS trusts and nationalised industries all pay real interest on their borrowing.

Notional interest acts as a charge on the capital, the total value of the assets, tied up in a public sector organisation. It will encourage the organisation to review and control the amount of capital it has. The rate that is charged varies - it may be 6% for statutory services (e.g. passports) and 8% or higher for non-statutory

services. In 1993 Ordnance Survey was charged notional interest at rates vary-
ing from 7.9%, an average rate for the year, on its average working capital, to
13.6% on land and buildings, the interest rate being that ruling on 1 April 1974,
the day the property was transferred to Ordnance Survey.

Free services

These are services which an organisation receives free of charge, the cost being
borne by another organisation. They are sometimes referred to as communicated costs. Common examples of intra-departmental free services are training,
personnel, internal audit and finance supplied from one part of a department to
another, perhaps an agency. Services provided free by another department are
known as allied services. These are notional costs only so far as they are not
actually charged (or hard charged). In arriving at the costs of the organisation
receiving the service a notional charge must be included. Another example of a
cost which government departments do not actually pay out is road fund licences for vehicles they operate.

One major service which government departments and agencies receive without making a payment is the external audit conducted by the National Audit
Office. Some organisations, such as trading funds, do have to pay for this service. Those who do not pay have to include a notional charge in their accounts.

❏ Nil cost

Items with nil cost do not usually appear in the accounts. Examples are the value
of staff loyalty and experience, where it would be very difficult to identify the
cost involved in acquiring such skills. This does mean that the accounts will not
contain a complete picture of the organisation. The Central Office of Information, a people based service organisation, shows its financial worth as only £2m,
yet achieves sales of around £120m each year.

❏ Full cost

This is the total cost to the organisation of providing its services. It will amount to:
Accruals costs - calculated on a modified historical or current cost basis - plus
notional costs.

References

Accounting Standards Committee
Accounting for the effect of changing prices : a Handbook
Institute of Chartered Accountants in England and Wales, London   1986

Advisory Group report to H M Treasury (Byatt Report)
Accounting for Economic Costs and Changing Prices
HMSO, London   1986

H M Treasury
Government Accounting
HMSO, London   1989 as amended

H M Treasury
Costing Guide
Unpublished   1992

H M Treasury
The Fees and Charges Guide
HMSO, London   1992

Walker
Principles of Cost Accounting
Macdonald and Evans, Plymouth   1982

Chapter 5

The operating account

Annual income twenty pounds, annual expenditure nineteen nineteen six, result happiness. Annual income twenty pounds, annual expenditure twenty pounds ought and six, result misery. (Mr Micawber in Oliver Twist, Charles Dickens)

Firstly, let us clear up some terminology. The operating account is, in fact, the same document as the:

- income and expenditure account
- expenditure account
- net expenditure account
- trading account
- memorandum trading account
- profit and loss account
- revenue account.

All of these terms cover the same document, with the same sort of information. The actual name used depends on the kind of organisation and whether it views its operations as being for profit. Examples of the terms used by different organisations are:

Operating account	Ordnance Survey
	HMSO
	Historic Royal Palaces
	Bank of England
	Forestry Commission
Income and expenditure account	National Physical Laboratory
	British Museum
	Remploy
	Independent Television Commission
	Scottish Hospital Trust
Net Expenditure Account	Chemical and Biological Defence Establishment

Trading account	Export Credit Guarantee Department
Memorandum trading account	Government Telecommunications Network
Profit and loss account	The Post Office
	British Coal
	London Transport
Revenue account	Crown Estate
and even -	
Cyfrif incwm a gwariant	S4C (Welsh Fourth Channel)
(Income and expenditure account)	CADW (Welsh Historic Monuments)

The elements of the operating account

The purpose of the operating account is to provide a record of the financial results for the period. It shows the income and costs. If there is more income than costs, the result will be a surplus (profit) and if there are more costs than income, or no income at all, there will be a deficit (loss). Public sector organisations very rarely use the terms 'profit' or 'loss' because the organisation does not usually exist to make profits, but to provide services. Each of the elements of the operating account will now be described in turn.

❏ Income

An organisation may have various types of income. These may be:

Trading income	from providing services or goods to other people or organisations
Grant received	from a sponsoring department
Investment income	earned on bank deposit accounts, government securities or other investments
Rental income	where property is rented out.

The main issue to be decided in working out how much income is to be included is the point in time at which the income is earned. For a service organisation, the income may be considered to be earned when the service has been completed. This may be before or after the point at which it is invoiced to the customer, or before or after the point at which the cash is received. For rental income, income could be included on the basis of the date on which the rent is due from the tenant. Alternatively the period which the rent covers could be used.

Some sources of receipts into an organisation will not be included as income. These are:

- receipts for sale of capital items which are no longer required
- receipts of grants to fund capital expenditure
- receipts of loan money.

Such receipts are not included in the operating account because they are not receipts in respect of income earned. (They will be included elsewhere in the accounts).

❑ Costs

The costs to be included in the operating account are those incurred in earning the income of the period, or, if there is no income, in providing the services for the period.

A common way of categorising costs, where there is significant trading activity, is first to identify the costs which relate directly to providing the goods or services. These are termed the 'cost of sales'. For an organisation buying and selling a product, cost of sales would be the cost of those items sold in the period. For a service organisation, cost of sales would be the cost of staff who are providing the service. The remaining costs can then be divided into 'other operating costs' and 'costs of finance', such as interest. If the organisation does not trade, then the costs may simply be classified by nature, e.g. staff costs, accommodation costs, if desired.

As the accounts are being prepared under the accruals convention, then care must be taken to ensure that the costs actually reflect the costs associated with activity during the period. These can be quite different from cash costs. For example, consider an organisation which buys and uses stationery. The basic information is as follows:

Opening stock of stationery at beginning of year	£40,000
Cash paid in year for stationery	£90,000
of which the figure related to stationery used in the previous year is	£5,000
Stationery invoiced and delivered to us, but not paid for at year end	£15,000
Stationery delivered to us, but not invoiced yet by supplier	£7,000
Closing stock of stationery at end of year	£20,000

So, what is the value of stationery consumed?

In this example, the cash figure of £90,000 has to be adjusted for stocks held at the beginning and end of the year, payments made in respect of previous periods and amounts owed for stationery.

The value of the stationery consumed is therefore:
$$40+90-5+15+7-20=127 \text{ (i.e. £127,000.)}$$

Other adjustments to cost items will be made for payments made in respect of following periods. If these are payments made in advance, then the prepaid amount will be deducted from this period's costs, and fall as a cost in the following period. In general, public bodies do not pay in advance of need, but there may be circumstances where this happens. Common examples are rents, maintenance contracts and travel tickets.

For example, assume that a computer maintenance contract runs from 1 July to 30 June. In year 1 the contract costs £4,000, and in year 2 it costs £6,000. The organisation pays each year on 1 July and its year end is 31 March. At the end of the year 3/12 will have been paid in advance. The cost for the accounting year needs to be adjusted from the cash amount of £6,000. This is shown in diagrammatic form in Figure 5.1.

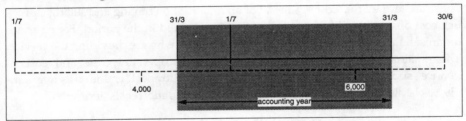

Figure 5.1 Prepaid contract.

The cost is thus $3/12 \times £4,000$ and $9/12 \times £6,000 = £5,500$.

If costs are not rising, then the effect of items paid regularly in advance and arrears will be neutral, and cash costs will be very close to accruals costs.

❏ Work in progress

For a service organisation, in working out the cost of the income it has earned, it needs to take into account any work in progress, i.e. where it has started work on a particular project, job, or contract but the work is not completed by the end of the accounting period. Such work cannot be included as income, even if the customer has already paid for it, because it is not completed. As the income will be recognised in the following period, then all the cost will also be carried over to the following period. This is in accordance with the accruals or matching principle that only the cost of delivering those services which have been included as income need to be included as costs.

❏ Depreciation

Where cash is paid out for an item which has a life of more than one year, it is not correct to charge the whole of the cash cost to the period in which the item is purchased as this would not reflect the cost of consuming the item. The cost should be spread over the expected useful life of the item, thus matching the cost to its consumption. The commonest way this is done is through depreciation.

Capital items

In order to examine this further, it is first necessary to decide which items count for this treatment. Such items are termed capital items, or fixed assets. There are various definitions of what should be classified as a capital item.

A capital item is defined by HM Treasury (1992) as:

> A tangible productive resource which is separately identifiable, of significant value and will yield a continuing service to the department in excess of one year.

The financial limit is not specified, and it is up to each organisation to choose an appropriate level. There is no requirement, for example, for the limit to be equal to that set by the Treasury for vote accounting purposes. One chair costing £50 would probably fail the test of being of significant value, whereas a £5,000 computer would pass.

Consider whether the following are capital or revenue expenditure?

1. £5,000 spent on window cleaning
2. £5,000 spent on double glazing
3. £5,000 spent on renting a photocopier
4. £5,000 spent on repairing a van after it crashed
5. £5,000 spent on computer hardware
6. £5,000 spent on a painting to hang in reception
7. £5,000 spent on 50 desks.

The window cleaning, photocopier and van repair would all be classified as revenue expenditure. With the photocopier, the organisation does not acquire more than the current year's use of the equipment. The van repair merely returns the van to the condition it was in before the crash, and does not increase the value of the van above its original value. The double glazing, computer hardware, painting and desks would be capital. The painting would be capital because it is productive in so far as it enhances the status of the organisation. If it was hanging in the chief executive's home it would probably not be. The desks comprise a significant amount together, even though each desk individually is not a high amount. Fixed assets are discussed in more detail in Chapter 6.

❑ The principle of depreciation

Once the decision has been made as to what is revenue and what is capital expenditure, then the capital items, the fixed assets, must have their cost spread over their expected useful life.

This is to reflect the fact that they lose value, because of:

- physical deterioration, caused by wear and tear, erosion, rust, rot or decay
- economic factors, such as obsolescence
- time factors, as with the expiry of leases and patents
- depletion, as in wasting assets such as mines, quarries and oil wells.

For example, a £10,000 van might have a 4-year life, and be depreciated at £2,500 a year. Each year £2,500 is charged as a cost of using the van. There would also be all the other costs such as fuel and servicing, which would be revenue expenditure and charged in the operating account.

In practice, depreciation can become rather more complicated. The £10,000 van might have a 4 year life, but instead of having no value at the end of its life, it might be expected to realise £1,000 in scrap or trade-in value at the end. The annual depreciation charge would then be calculated as:

$$\frac{\text{Cost less estimated residual value}}{\text{Estimated useful life}} = \frac{£10,000 - £1,000}{4} = £2,250$$

This method of charging depreciation is called the straight line method, because an equal amount will be charged in each of the 4 years, a graph of the depreciation charge can be seen in Figure 5.2.

Depreciation methods

The straight line method is the simplest and commonest but there are others. Three such methods are described below. The first is the reducing balance method. This charges depreciation as a constant percentage of the net value of the fixed asset.

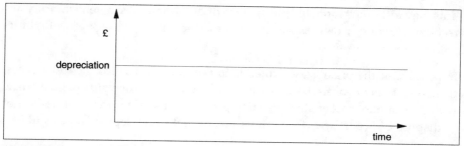

Figure 5.2 Straight line depreciation.

This results in a charge, for the same £10,000 van, which approximates to:

Year 1	£10,000	at 45%	4,500
Year 2	£5,500	at 45%	2,475
Year 3	£3,025	at 45%	1,361
Year 4	£1,664	at 45%	749
Total			9,085

The rate of 45% does not write off exactly £9,000 over the four years. The actual formula to use, to arrive at the correct rate is:

$$R = 100 \left(1 - \sqrt[n]{\frac{x}{y}} \right)$$

where R = percentage rate, n = life, x = residual value and y = cost.

This would work out as:

$$R = 100 \left(1 - \sqrt[4]{\frac{1,000}{10,000}} \right) = 43.77\%$$

This method gives a much higher charge in the early years. A graph of the charge would be as shown in Figure 5.3.

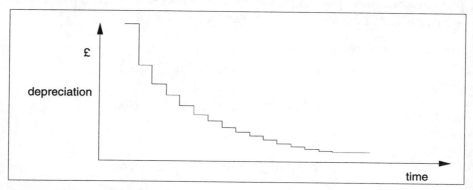

Figure 5.3 Reducing balance depreciation.

41

This may feel much more like the pattern of depreciation on a vehicle which we recognise from our own experience of new cars. The vehicle loses a lot of its value in the first year.

In practice, if the organisation intends to keep the vehicle for the full 4 years, then, on a going concern basis, it does not matter what the value of the vehicle would be on the market at intervening points in time, since the intention is not to dispose of it part way through its life. Straight line depreciation would be acceptable.

Once the likely servicing and repair costs for the van are added to the cost of depreciation calculated according to the reducing balance method, then the total cost (apart from fuel, insurance and road tax) of owning and operating the vehicle's can be calculated. This may give an approximately even charge throughout the vehicle's life as seen in Figure 5.4; the distance from the horizontal to the step-line shows the depreciation cost, the distance from the step-line to the total cost line shows the cost of servicing and repairs.

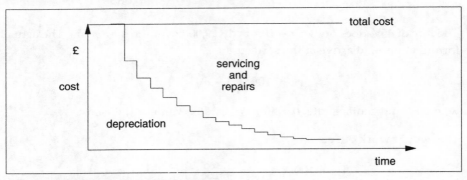

Figure 5.4.Total costs of running a vehicle.

A second option is to use what is known as the sum of the digits method. This method would be applied to the £10,000 van with a 4-year life, and the total life would be taken from the number of years as $4 + 3 + 2 + 1 = 10$.

The depreciation charges would be:

$$\text{Year 1} \quad 10,000 - 1,000 \times \tfrac{4}{10} = 3,600$$

$$\text{Year 2} \quad 10,000 - 1,000 \times \tfrac{3}{10} = 2,700$$

$$\text{Year 3} \quad 10,000 - 1,000 \times \tfrac{2}{10} = 1,800$$

$$\text{Year 4} \quad 10,000 - 1,000 \times \tfrac{1}{10} = 900$$

$$\text{Total} = 9,000$$

This method is a reasonable approximation to the reducing balance method and is easier to calculate than using the precise reducing balance formula.

A third method is to base the depreciation charge on some measure of consumption. Machinery may have a manufacturer's specification for the number of units it will produce, vehicles may be traded in after a specified number of miles and planes may have an expected life in flying hours. The charge for each year could be based on the units, miles or hours in that year compared to the total that can be expected over the life of the asset.

Choice of cost and life

In all the calculations of depreciation, there is the choice of which cost figure to use, i.e. the historical or current. This was discussed fully in Chapter 4. The choice of expected useful life will also affect the depreciation charge. Choices on the asset lives are discussed in Chapter 6. The decision on how much depreciation to charge in the year of purchase - nil, full year or pro rata to ownership, must also be made. The depreciation charge will only be an approximation for the cost of using the fixed asset. No-one can predict that the vehicle will last exactly 4 years, and that the scrap value will be exactly £1,000.

The predictions will be based on past experience, and will give costs that should be materially correct. If not enough depreciation has been charged before disposal, then there will be a loss on disposal to charge to the operating account in the year of disposal.

❑ Bad debts

Bad debts arise as a result of making sales on credit and also using accruals accounting, which includes income when it is earned, rather than when the money is received from the customer. Under cash accounting, bad debts do not explicitly appear in the accounts. The income will simply not have been included in the first place as no cash had been received. Under either accounting method, however, the effect of bad debts on the organisation is the same, in that it does not collect cash to which it is entitled.

Under accruals accounting, the operating account needs to show separately the amount earned from customers, and the bad debt cost. Problems with the amounts the organisation is due to receive can arise for a number of reasons, perhaps because the customers are in financial difficulties or because they are disputing the quality of the services or goods they received. Under the prudence concept the operating account should show the bad debts as a cost for the period, as soon as it is recognised that the customers may not or will not pay. This cost is shown as a separate expense, not as a deduction from sales. If it were deducted from sales, this would hide the cost of doing business with the wrong sort of customers.

❏ Provisions

The need to allow for provisions also arises from the prudence concept. These costs are included even though the exact amount and time of payment are not known.

Examples are:

- redundancy and restructuring costs
- early retirement cost
- major repairs
- compensation claims.

These costs are provided for in full in the operating account as soon as they are recognised as being likely to occur, even though the actual cash may not be paid out for some years. They can be a fruitful ground for creative accounting as described in Chapter 11.

❏ Exceptional items

Exceptional items are defined (Accounting Standards Board 1993) as:

> material items which derive from events or transactions that fall within the ordinary activities of the reporting entity and which individually or, if of a similar type, in aggregate, need to be disclosed by virtue of their size or incidence if the financial statements are to give a true and fair view.

Exceptional items include material charges for bad debts and gains and losses on sale of assets. Material provisions (as described above) may be shown as exceptional items. Separate disclosure prevents these items being subsumed in other headings in the accounts.

❏ Preparation of operating account

The following example demonstrates the preparation of a simple operating account. The basic information is shown in Figure 5.5.

Under accruals accounting the operating account would appear as in Figure 5.6.

It may be useful to contrast this document with the presentation of the results under cash accounting rules. This is shown in Figure 5.7.

For someone managing or monitoring Book Selling Enterprises, it is more informative to have an operating account, which states that the organisation has made a surplus of £3,500, rather than a cash account which states that £73,000 has been paid out and nothing received. The cash must always be monitored, and will be reported in the cash flow statement, as discussed in Chapter 7.

Book Selling Enterprises

Book Selling Enterprises, a small public sector organisation, starts up on 1 April 1994 and has the following transactions during the 6 months ended 30 September 1994:

- £100,000 loan received and paid into bank account
  The loan bears interest at 6%, payable at the end of each year

- Cash Payments   £15,000   running costs – staff, fuel, utilities, rent, consumables

                      £8,000   delivery van

                  £10,000   furniture

                  £40,000   leasehold premises (10 year lease)

- Cash receipts from trading   £ NIL

- Sales transactions for which cash has not yet been received   £40,000

- Books purchased, but cash not paid   £25,000

- Cost of books left in stock at 30 September   £10,000

Figure 5.5. Book Selling Enterprises

Book Selling Enterprises

Operating account for the 6 months to 30 September 1994

	£	£
Sales		40,000
Cost of sales:		
purchases	25,000	
less closing stock	10,000	
		15,000
Gross surplus		25,000
Expenses:		
Administration expenses	15,000	
Depreciation:		
Vehicle (25% per annum)	1,000	
Furniture (10% per annum)	500	
Leasehold premises	2,000	
Interest	3,000	
		21,500
Net surplus		£ 3,500

Note ~ the depreciation periods for the vehicle and furniture are assumptions.

Figure 5.6. Book Selling Enterprises operating account.

Book Selling Enterprises

Cash account for the 6 months to 30 September 1994

	£
Payments:	
Running Costs	15,000
Capital	58,000
	73,000
Receipts	–
Net total	73,000

Figure 5.7. Book Selling Enterprises cash account.

Examples of operating accounts

The operating account of Ordnance Survey is shown in Figure 5.8.

Ordnance Survey
Operating Account
for the Year Ended 31 March 1993   All amounts are in £ thousands

	Note	1992/93	1991/92
Turnover	2	49 027	48 726
Change in stocks of finished goods			
and work in progress		(1 239)	381
Raw materials and consumables		(1 651)	(1 611)
Other external charges		(12 478)	(10 609)
Staff costs	3	(45 874)	(44 996)
Amortisation of intangible fixed assets		–	
Depreciation of tangible fixed assets	(3 885)		
plus loss on sale of fixed assets	(51)	(3 936)	(4 168)
Other operating charges		(6 447)	(7 276)
Operating Deficit	4	(22 598)	(19 553)
Exceptional Item	5	(24 365)	–
Deficit before interest on capital		(46 963)	(19 553)
Interest on capital	1.11	(3 150)	(3 610)
Deficit for year on operations		(50 113)	(23 163)

Figure 5.8. Ordnance Survey operating account.

The brackets all over this operating account just reflect the fact that Ordnance Survey makes a deficit and relies on vote finance to cover this deficit and make ends meet. The figures in brackets are either costs or deficits.

The costs are here listed together, rather than being split between cost of sales and expenses. The costs exceed the turnover, and the operating deficit is made greater by the exceptional item. The note to the accounts (not shown here) explains that this is made up of provisions for early retirement and future pension costs. There is then an interest charge - a notional charge because Ordnance Survey has not actually borrowed funds from anyone.

The operating account for HMSO is shown in Figure 5.9.

HMSO
Historic Cost Operating Account
For The Year Ended 31 December 1993

	Notes	1993 £000	£000	1992 £000	£000
Turnover		360,083		371,122	
Change in stocks of:					
finished goods		1,364		(536)	
work in progress		1,945		(6,382)	
Government grants	3	3,380		2,562	
Other operating income		2,383		2,875	
			369,155		369,641
Raw materials and consumables		6,425		16,224	
Other external charges		241,381		239,946	
Staff costs	7	76,748		70,961	
Depreciation	4	5,545		5,616	
Other operating charges		35,169		29,462	
			365,268		362,209
Operating surplus	2/4		3,887		7,432
Net interest receivable	8		1,264		1,018
Surplus on ordinary activities			5,151		8,450
Interest payable on long–term loans	9		1,018		1,575
Retained surplus for year	19c		4,133		6,875

Figure 5.9 HMSO operating account.

This operating account looks much healthier than Ordnance Survey's, not just because the costs are not put in brackets. HMSO has three sources of income - turnover for goods and services is the largest. It has a diminishing government grant - a vote for supplying publications to public libraries at half price.

The highest costs are other external charges, which are for work carried out for HMSO by subcontractors. HMSO earned £1m actual interest on overnight balances.

After paying actual interest on its loans, HMSO is left with a surplus of £4m, lower than that of the previous year, with a lower turnover.

HMSO also produces a set of current cost accounts, following the method set out in Chapter 4. These show that the surplus is increased by £328,000, the different costs under CCA being:

	£000
Supplementary depreciation	134
Fixed asset disposals	(27)
Cost of sales	(516)
Monetary working capital	81
	(328)

Other examples of operating accounts are included in Chapter 8.

Continuing and discontinued operations

The operating accounts looked at so far have been simple in that they are presenting information for an organisation which has remained structurally stable over the accounting period. Where an organisation is made up of a number of bodies, as with a group of companies, then it is possible for there to be changes in the period, with parts of the organisation leaving and others joining.

If this has happened, then Financial Reporting Standard 3 (ASB 1993) states that the operating account must be analysed to show the effect. Different layouts may achieve this purpose - an example is:

	Continuing operations	Acquisitions	Discontinued operations	Total
	£	£	£	£
Turnover	100	50	20	170
Cost of sales	40	20	10	70
Gross surplus	60	30	10	100
Operating costs	20	10	20	50
Operating surplus	40	20	(10)	50
Interest				10
Net surplus				40

This is intended to enable a user of the accounts to predict the future results of the organisation with more accuracy.

References

Accounting Standards Board
Financial Reporting Standard 3
ASB, London   1993

H M Treasury
Accounting for Capital Assets: A Working Draft of Guidance
Unpublished   1992

Chapter 6

The balance sheet

Creditors have better memories than debtors (Howell, 1659)

Whereas the operating account shows the performance of an organisation over a specified period, the purpose of the balance sheet is to provide a financial picture of the affairs of an organisation at one point in time. It shows the resources controlled by the organisation. The balance sheet is forced to balance because of the fundamental accounting equation, which states that:

Assets less liabilities equals capital

or, in plain English,

What we own, less what we owe, equals what we are worth.

Assets

Assets are things that are worth something to the organisation. The strict definition from the Accounting Standards Board is

rights or other access to future economic benefits controlled by an entity as a result of past transactions or events.

Assets are classified as either fixed or current assets depending on their nature.

❏ Fixed assets

These are defined by the Accounting Standards Board as those assets which are intended for use on a continuing basis in the enterprise's activities (SSAP 12). They represent unexpired capital expenditure. The common types of fixed asset that are likely to occur are:

- land and buildings - freehold and leasehold
- computers
- office equipment
- vehicles
- furniture
- plant and equipment.

For specialised organisations, there are specialised fixed assets, such as:

- locomotives (British Rail)
- ships (Natural Environment Research Council)
- aircraft (Civil Aviation Authority)
- trees (Forestry Commission)
- mines (British Coal)
- investment properties (Crown Estate)
- art collection (Arts Council)
- medical equipment (NHS Hospital Trusts)
- film library (Central Office of Information).

These assets are classified as fixed because the aim of owning them is not to sell them but to keep them for the long term use of the organisation.

Any fixed asset could be sold at any time, albeit for a reduced price. Using the going concern basis of preparing the accounts, the assumption is made that the items classified as fixed assets will be kept to the end of their normal useful lives. Only if circumstances change, and disposal is imminent, would fixed assets be reclassified as current.

Organisations can survive very successfully with no fixed assets. If an organisation chooses to rent furnished premises, and to hire in computers and vehicles as and when needed, then it will not show any fixed assets on its balance sheet.

❏ Valuation of fixed assets

The value included in the balance sheet depends on :

- the cost attributed to the asset - historical, current or other
- the estimated useful life
- the method of depreciation used, e.g. straight line.

The choice of costs was discussed in Chapter 4 and asset lives and depreciation methods were covered in Chapter 5.

The simplest method of valuing fixed assets is to use the cost less accumulated depreciation.There are also some specialised methods of valuing fixed assets:

Net recoverable amount: the greater of the estimated net present value of the cash flows deriving from the continued use of the asset, and the estimated net proceeds of disposal of the asset. This method is used by the Defence Research Agency for valuing major facilities.

Modern equivalent asset value: the estimated current replacement cost of the assets, adjusted for service potential less accumulated depreciation. This is used by the BBC on plant and machinery.

❑ Asset lives

There are no rules laid down, either from the Accounting Standards Board or from the Treasury, on what lives should be used for different categories of fixed assets. The choice lies with each organisation preparing its accounts, and should be made to reflect the reality of how long the fixed assets actually last in that organisation.

The following examples, selected from 1993 accounts, give an indication of the ranges of asset lives in use.

Freehold land

Freehold land is normally not depreciated, because it has an infinite life. However, Ordnance Survey includes a downwards revaluation and British Coal depreciates land used as dirt tips. The reasons for this are that it is considered that the land has suffered a permanent fall in value.

Freehold buildings	*Years*
Defence Research Agency	20
Hanover Housing Association, Patent Office	40
Arts Council, BBC, Royal Mint, British Coal	50
Remploy, Ordnance Survey	60
Vehicle Inspectorate	17 - 40
Forestry Commission	20 - 80
British Museum	20 - 112
Post Office	up to 60

Properties acquired and owned primarily for investment purposes are not required to be depreciated. The accounts of the Bank of England, the Crown Estate and Hanover Housing Association show properties which are treated in this way.

Leasehold buildings

The cost of the lease is usually amortised over the remainder of the lease. Amortisation is identical to depreciation, except that the term amortisation is used only in respect of intangible assets. Here the buildings are not intangible, but the lease is.

There are some examples of exceptions to the normal treatment. These include the following:

Post Office   either the period of the lease, 60 years or the valuer's estimate of the remaining useful life

Independent Television Commission   the lesser of the term of the lease or 50 years

Remploy   the period of lease or 50 years, whichever is shorter

These all reflect the application of prudence, in not extending the life beyond either that used for freehold buildings, or the actual life of the lease.

Computers	*Years*
The Buying Agency	up to 3
Crown Estate	4
ITC, BBC, Vehicle Inspectorate	5
National Physical Laboratory	7
Bank of England	3 - 5
Post Office	3 - 6
Companies House	3 - 7

In the case of computers, obsolescence is potentially a very important factor in determining the asset life. They are very often scrapped in favour of a newer model, even though they are not physically worn out.

Office equipment	*Years*
Defence Research Agency	3
Patent Office, The Buying Agency, National Physical Laboratory }	5

Vehicles	*Years*
Arts Council	4
Ordnance Survey	2 - 8
BBC	7 - 10
Central Office of Information	5 - 13

Plant and equipment	*Years*
Companies House	4 - 10
Royal Mint	10 - 20

Assets in the course of construction, such as partly constructed buildings, are not depreciated until they have been completed and are in use.

❏ Leased assets

In addition to fixed assets which the organisation has bought, there may be assets which are leased. This is not as common in the public sector as it is in the private sector. However, leases are frequently taken out for buildings, vehicles, and equipment such as photocopiers, where the leasing costs are significantly lower than the cost of purchase. It is necessary to decide whether to treat the leased item as a fixed asset or a rental.

If it is a fixed asset, it counts as a finance lease, effectively belonging to the lessee (following the substance over form concept,) and will be included on the balance sheet, with depreciation and interest charged on the operating account. If it is treated as a rented asset all of the lease payment will be treated as an expense in the operating account.

The criteria for classifying the lease as a finance lease and capitalising the asset are set out in SSAP 21. This states that a lease is a finance lease if it transfers substantially all the risks and rewards of ownership of an asset to the lessee.

❏ Intangible fixed assets

There are certain items which are included as fixed assets, despite the fact that there is no tangible object. Examples are:

- patents
- licences
- computer software
- copyright.

Where these are owned by the organisation, and of value, they will be included on the balance sheet. Where the value is nil, or uncertain, then the application of the prudence concept means that they will not appear. Examples of those which are included are:

Horserace Totalisator Board	betting office licences £16m (out of balance sheet total £36m), not depreciated.
BBC	investments in programmes for future sale £45m (out of £833m total), carried forward until programmes sold.
Patent Office	deferred relocation costs £7m (out of £17m total) written off over 5 years (reducing balance 50%).

Vehicle Inspectorate   computer software, depreciated over 6 years.

Assets which do exist but are not included on the balance sheet are discussed below.

❏ Investments

Investments are usually monetary holdings in another organisation, such as shares. Investments will be classified as fixed assets if they are intended to be held for the long term. Short term investments will count as current assets, which are considered overleaf.

The types of investments which appear in public sector balance sheets are:

- shares
- loans
- Government securities
- charity investment funds
- antiques and paintings (Crown Estate).

❏ Current assets

All assets are either fixed or current, so if an asset exists and is not a fixed asset, it must be a current asset. The categories of current assets are:

- stock and work in progress
- debtors and prepayments
- investments and loans
- bank and cash.

Each of these is described separately below.

Current assets exist because the organisation takes some time to complete the service or goods it is delivering and therefore has money tied up in items which will eventually work their way through the cycle to turn into cash. This is shown in Figure 6.1.

❏ Stock and work in progress

Stock may include any of:

- raw materials
- work in progress of manufactured goods
- work in progress of services
- finished goods
- consumables (such as heating oil or stationery).

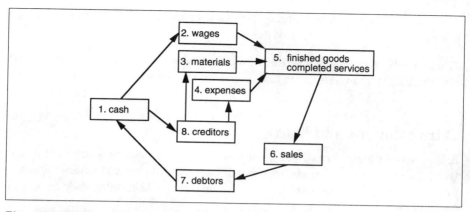

Figure 6.1 The flow of money through an organisation.

The general guidance of the prudence concept, in not anticipating gains, but anticipating losses, means that stock is valued at the lower of cost and net realisable value. An example is given in Figure 6.2.

Stock item	Cost	Estimated selling price	Estimated cost to complete	Net realisable value	Value in accounts
	1	*2*	*3*	*4 (2–3)*	*lower of 1 and 4*
A	1,000	1,500	300	1,200	1,000
B	1,000	1,500	600	900	900
Total	2,000	3,000	900	2,100	1,900

Figure 6.2 Stock valuation

Here it can be seen that the value in the accounts must be calculated for each item separately, rather than for the items together. It may be necessary to make provisions for obsolete and damaged stock, or for irrecoverable work in progress.

❑ Debtors and prepayments

The assets that are included here are:

- trade debtors (customers who owe money)
- sundry debtors, e.g. staff travel advances
- prepayments, e.g. rent paid in advance
- recoverable VAT.

The trade debtors will be valued following prudence, ie at invoice value less provisions for bad and doubtful debts.

There may be debtors who are due to pay after more than one year. These amounts will be disclosed on a separate line on the balance sheet , though still as current assets.

❑ Investments and loans

Examples of investments were given earlier. If long term, they are included in fixed assets. Short term investments will be similar items, but where the intention of the organisation is to dispose of them within 12 months they are classified as current assets.

❑ Bank and cash

Money held in bank accounts and in cash form is included here. Bank overdrafts are not netted off against bank balances, but are shown in liabilities.

❑ Assets not on the balance sheet

There are many things that a public sector organisation may possess which do not appear on the balance sheet. These may be tangible or intangible items. Examples of items which exist and are not included in the balance sheet are given below.

Tangible items

Royal Mint: 'no account is taken of the Royal Mint collection of coins and medals which is of inestimable value.'

British Museum : 'the value of artefacts forming the collections is considered to be incalculable, and no amount is included in the Balance Sheet.'

Historic Royal Palaces: 'title to the freehold land and buildings of the palaces is held by the Crown. No valuation of the estate, historic fabric of the buildings or historic objects has been included in the accounts.'

University of St Andrews: the balance sheet totals £46m, but collections of books, art and silver of £75m are not included.

Ordnance Survey: stocks of large scale maps are not included - the accounts are qualified by the National Audit Office as a result (see Chapter 9).

Intangible items

Ordnance Survey: 'no value for the National Topographic Database appears in the Balance Sheet.'

Companies House: capitalised development project expenditure on computer based registers was previously carried forward in the balance sheet, and in 1993 was written off in full as a £2m cost in the operating account.

Land Registry: no value is included for the land register.

Many of these items are not included because they are managed, but effectively not controlled, by the organisation. They are irreplaceable, and would never be for sale. Other items which do not appear on a balance sheet are intangibles such as the value of staff loyalty and experience, and the customers.

Certain assets, which have appreciated in value but where prudence does not allow the inclusion of the higher value, can show the higher value in a note to the accounts. An example would be fixed asset investments held, which are shown at cost with a note disclosing current market value.

Liabilities

Liabilities are money owed by the organisation. They are defined by the Accounting Standards Board as:

> an entity's obligations to transfer economic benefits as a result of past transactions or events.

Liabilities are classified as either long term or current, depending on how long it is before they are due to be paid. Liabilities which are very remote are classified as provisions.

❏ Current liabilities

These are due to be paid within 12 months of the balance sheet date. The common categories are:

- trade creditors (suppliers)
- capital creditors
- other creditors
- accruals (services received but not yet invoiced)
- loans
- PAYE (income tax,) national insurance, VAT
- deferred income (where customers pay in advance)
- bank overdrafts

- pension commitments
- finance leases
- salaries and wages.

Current liabilities which are less common include:

- corporation tax - for those organisations which are liable, including ITC, S4C, Bank of England, nationalised industries
- public deposits - the Bank of England
- proposed dividend - Companies House, Royal Mint
- money due to be surrendered to the Consolidated Fund - Forestry Commission, Ordnance Survey, the Buying Agency
- unpresented cheques - BBC.

❑ Long-term liabilities

Long-term liabilities are those which are due for payment more than 12 months after the balance sheet date. They include items such as:

- loans
- redundancy, early retirement and pension commitments
- trade creditors
- finance leases.

❑ Provisions

Provisions are amounts set aside for costs which are not yet known. An example would be provisions for redundancy costs, where the decision to make staff redundant has been taken before the end of the accounting period, but the actual costs will be paid out in following years.

Other examples are:

- insurance
- restructuring
- income tax liability for past and present employees
- early retirement.

In the case of British Coal, provisions have been made for pensions, concessionary fuel, surface damage, site restoration, post-closure and related costs, insurance and noise induced hearing loss. These totalled £2,431m and reduced the balance sheet net assets total to £611m at 27 March 1993.

There may well be a potential overlap between long-term liabilities and provisions, as in the case of redundancy costs, and each organisation will need to decide how firm the liability is when deciding where to include it.

❏ Liabilities not on the balance sheet

The balance sheet will only include known liabilities in respect of items where goods or services have been received by the organisation by the end of the accounting period. It will therefore exclude:

Contingent liabilities: where the probability of the liability falling due is very remote

Commitments: where an order has been placed for expenses or fixed assets.

Contingent liabilities and capital commitments will be disclosed in notes to the accounts.

Contingent liabilities

Examples of some contingent liabilities in public sector accounts are:

- guarantees to relocation companies in respect of staff house moves - Patent Office
- guarantees, outstanding litigation, indemnities and contractual arrangements: British Rail £156m, compared to balance sheet net assets £2,325m at 31 March 1993
- negligence claim: Vehicle Inspectorate £260,000, compared to balance sheet £36m
- deferred taxation: Civil Aviation Authority £34m compared to balance sheet £433m
- potential claims for nuclear damage, insurance cover, restructuring, decommissioning and radioactive waste management, premature retirement, non-radioactive chemical groundwater contamination: Atomic Energy Authority

Capital commitments

Information must be shown on the amounts authorised and contracted for at the year end.

Capital

This is the third part of the equation - assets less liabilities equals capital. It is intended to answer the question:

Where did we get the money for what we have?

Capital in the private sector is usually made up of two components, share capital and reserves where reserves, in effect, mean past profits. In the public sector, there are many different ways of showing where the organisation got the funds to acquire the net assets.

The most common components are:

Revaluation reserve: this reflects the fact that the value of the fixed assets in the other half of the balance sheet is at net replacement cost, and hence has moved away from the historical cost actually paid;

Retained surplus/income and expenditure account/ profit and loss account: all the net surpluses and deficits since the organisation was set up, (or since it started preparing accruals accounts.)

One complication arises because different names are sometimes used to mean the same thing. Retained surplus is also called:

General Fund: by Ordnance Survey, Historic Royal Palaces

General Reserve: by Bank of England, The Buying Agency , Patent Office

Revenue Reserve: by Crown Estates

Other items found include:

Capital account/ reserve	is used by National Physical Laboratory, Arts Council, BBC, London Transport, to describe funds already used for capital spend
Public Dividend Capital	used by trading funds, such as Patent Office, and NHS trusts, to describe the notional shareholding held by the Consolidated Fund
Capital (bank stock)	used by Bank of England to describe shares in the organisation
Vested capital	London Transport has the capital with which it was set up in 1970
Grant-in-aid	Forestry Commission shows the cumulative Grant-in-aid in the current 3-year period

Funds which the organisation has received, or has earmarked for a particular use are described as:

- Purchase fund and building fund: British Museum
- Endowment fund: Scottish Hospital Trust
- Special reserve: Patent Office and Hanover Housing

Other items may be:

- Deferred grants: where a fixed asset has been partly or wholly financed by a grant

The term *'Reserves'* is sometimes used to cover one or more of the above, and an analysis of the notes to the accounts will explain which are involved.

Preparation of balance sheet

Continuing the same example which was started in Chapter 5, the balance sheet for Book Selling Enterprises will appear as in Figure 6.3.

Book Selling Enterprises Balance sheet at 30 September 1994	£	£
Assets		
Leasehold premises		38,000
Vehicle		7,000
Furniture		9,500
		54,500
Stock	10,000	
Debtors	40,000	
Bank	27,000	
	77,000	
Less: Creditors	28,000	
		49,000
Net assets		£103,500
Funded by		
Loan		100,000
Surplus		3,500
		£103,500

Figure 6.3 Balance sheet – Book Selling Enterprises.

This is the most common layout for a balance sheet. It is equally possible to balance it with liabilities and capital on the left hand side, and assets on the right, but very few organisations prepare their balance sheets in that way.

❏ Examples of balance sheets

Ordnance Survey

Ordnance Survey
Balance Sheet
at 31 March 1993

All amounts are in £ thousands

	Note	31 March 1993		31 March 1992
Fixed assets				
Intangible assets	9.1	–		
Tangible assets	9.2	**34 350)**	34 350	37 346
Current assets				
Loan: 1–5 years	10	1		32
Stocks & work in progress	11	4 331		
Debtors	12	10 214		10 957
Cash at bank and in hand	13	2 017		3 692
		16 563		20 427
Creditors: amounts falling due within one year	14	(7 404)		(8 091)
Net current assets			9 159	12 336
Total assets *less* current liabilities			43 509	49 682
Amounts falling due after one year	15	(23 777)		–
Net assets			19 732	49 682
Financed by:				
Capital and reserves				
General fund			4 692	31 100
Revaluation reserve	16		15 040	18 582
			19 732	49 682

The notes on pages 21 to 28 form part of these accounts
The accounts were approved on 1 July 1993

David W Rhind Accounting Officer

The top half of the Ordnance Survey balance sheet contains common items. There is one significant change from 1992, with the £23,777,000 under 'amounts falling due after more than one year'. This represents the provision for early retirement and pension commitments which have been recognised this year for the first time.

The 'Financed by' half of the balance sheet shows a large fall in the general fund - this reflects the deficit for the year, and the largest item causing this deficit is the provision. There is also a fall in the revaluation reserve, reflecting the fact that the fixed assets have been revalued down compared to 1992. This is mainly due to the fall in the value of land and buildings.

HMSO

HMSO
Historical Cost Balance Sheet
As at 31 December 1993

	Notes	31 December 1993 £000	£000	31 December 1992 £000	£000
Fixed assets					
Tangible assets	10a		44,273		48,616
Current assets					
Stocks	11	27,499		22,219	
Debtors	12	51,483		56,124	
Cash at bank and in hand	13	7,465		5,341	
		86,447		83,684	
Creditors					
Amounts falling due within one year	14	(62,764)		(62,410)	
Net current assets			23,683		21,274
Total assets less current liabilities			67,956		69,890
Amounts falling due after one year	15		(5,477)		(3,086)
Net assets			62,479		66,804
Financed by:					
Provision for insurance	19a		6,000		6,000
Capital and reserves					
National Loans Fund	18	1,669		5,008	
Revaluation reserve	19b	3,262		8,381	
Retained surplus	19c	51,548		47,415	
			56,479		60,804
			62,479		66,804

PAUL I FREEMAN
Accounting Officer

13 April 1994
The notes on pages 20 to 31 form an integral part of these accounts.

This balance sheet shows the standard headings in the top half. The 'amounts falling due after one year' of £5,477,000 are finance lease obligations and pension commitments.

The lower half includes HMSO's own insurance fund, as HMSO is a trading fund and not covered by the general government self-insurance pool. Part of the loans has been paid off - it appears that in another year they will all have been repaid. The revaluation reserve has also fallen, by a much higher amount than Ordnance Survey but for the same reasons.

The increase in the retained surplus corresponds to the £4,133,000 at the foot of the operating account which was shown in Chapter 5.

❏ Statement of total recognised gains and losses

The purpose of this statement is to highlight all the gains and losses that have been recognised in the accounting period, including gains and losses which have not actually passed through the operating account as realised items. Examples of gains and losses which are recognised but not realised are:

- revaluation of fixed assets
- foreign exchange gains and losses.

BBC
Statement of Total Recognised Gains and Losses
for the year ended 31 March

	1992/93	1991/92
	£m	£m
Deficit for the financial year	(26.8)	(24.8)
Unrealised surplus on revaluation of plant and machinery	80.5	–
Currency translation differences on foreign currency net investments	1.3	–
Total recognised gains and losses relating to the year	55.0	(24.8)

In this case, the BBC made a deficit for each year on its activities as reported in the operating account.

Although this is a simple statement, it should be given the same emphasis of presentation as the operating account and balance sheet.

References

Accounting Standards Board
Draft Statement of Principles
ASB, London   1992

Accounting Standards Committee
SSAP12
ICAEW, London   1987

Chapter 7

Cash flow statement

Ah, take the cash and let the credit go (Edward Fitzgerald, Omar Khayyám)

Although the accounts are prepared on the accruals basis, the importance of the underlying cash flow cannot be forgotten. More private sector businesses fail for lack of cash than because they are unprofitable. The purpose of the cash flow statement is to provide information on the way the organisation has generated and absorbed cash in the period. It should assist the users of the accounts in their assessment of the liquidity, viability and financial adaptability of the organisation. The need to provide information on the cash picture arises because an organisation may appear, from the operating account, to be performing well, and the balance sheet may also appear healthy, but the cash flow statement may reveal a very different picture. An organisation may run out of cash if it 'overtrades', i.e. generates more activity but the cash fails to move quickly enough round the cycle shown in Figure 6.1.

Structure of the cash flow statement

The cash flow statement reconciles the difference between the amount of cash (and cash equivalents) at the beginning of the period and at the end. It does this by analysing what has caused the movements into the following five categories:

- operating activities
- returns on investments and servicing of finance
- taxation
- investing activities
- financing.

❏ Operating activities

This part of the statement takes the operating surplus and adjusts for items not involving the movement of cash. The amount of cash flowing into or out of the organisation as a result of operating activities can be calculated by adding together the following items and deducting those shown in brackets:

- operating surplus or (deficit)

- depreciation
- notional costs
- (surplus) or deficit on disposal of fixed assets
- (increase) or decrease in stocks
- (increase) or decrease in debtors
- increase or (decrease) in creditors.

Starting with the value of the operating surplus, adjusting for each item will result in an increase or decrease in the cash that was generated from operating activities. Each of these is either a non-cash item (such as depreciation) or an item where there is more or less cash available (such as an increase in debtors which would result in less cash.)

❏ Returns on investments and servicing of finance

This groups together the amounts actually received and paid in cash (as opposed to amounts earned or incurred) on investments and servicing of finance. Examples are:

- bank interest received
- loan interest paid
- interest on finance leases
- dividends paid
- Consolidated Fund payment.

❏ Taxation

This will show the amount of tax paid, rather than the tax charged in the accounts. The main component will be Corporation Tax, for the organisations who are subject to it. VAT which merely passes through the organisation will be ignored for the cash flow statement. Any amount owed or owing at the balance sheet date will appear on the balance sheet as a creditor or debtor. Some organisations cannot reclaim all the VAT that they incur. Such irrecoverable VAT will not be treated as taxation, but be included with the cost to which it belongs, usually as part of operating activities or the purchase of fixed assets.

❏ Investing activities

There are two categories of activities here. One is investment in intangibles, i.e. financial investments. The other is money invested in tangible fixed assets such as land and buildings or equipment. Separate information is provided on the cash flowing into investments, and the cash released by disposing of investments. The headings, with some specific examples from particular public sector organisations, are:

- payments to acquire tangible fixed assets
- receipts from sale of tangible fixed assets
- sale of investments
- repayment of relocation creditor (Patent Office)
- investments in programmes for future sale (BBC)
- purchase of subsidiary undertaking (Atomic Energy Authority)
- purchase of gilt edged securities (Crown Estates.)

If the organisation has received a grant to fund part or all of the fixed asset purchase, then the fixed asset is included here at its gross amount, and the grant is included under financing activities.

❏ Financing

This relates to the receipt of cash from issuing finance, or the payment of cash to redeem finance. Examples are:

- loans received
- repayments of loans (in whole or by instalments)
- government grant received
- net vote expenditure appropriated
- Public Dividend Capital issued.

The analysis of all the movements into these five categories will cover all the different ways in which the cash may flow into or out of the organisation. Any one organisation may not have cash flows resulting from all the categories. When all five are added together, the net movement will exactly match the increase or decrease in cash and cash equivalents over the period. Cash equivalents comprise short term investments, which will become cash within three months of the balance sheet date.

For organisations which receive some or all of their funds in cash from Government funds, as vote finance or grant-in-aid, then the cash flow statement allows a useful reconciliation back to the information provided in cash accounts.

Preparation of cash flow statement

If we consider Book Selling Enterprises again, then its cash flow statement will be constructed as follows in Figures 7.1. and 7.2.

Book Selling Enterprises
Cash flow from operating activities:

	£
Surplus before interest	6,500
Depreciation	3,500
Increase in stocks	(10,000)
Increase in debtors	(40,000)
Increase in creditors	25,000
Outflow of cash	£ (15,000)

Figure 7.1 Book Selling Enterprises, Cash flow from operating activities

---

Book Selling Enterprises
Cash flow statement for the 6 months to 30 September 1994

	£
Net cash outflow from operating activities	(15,000)
Return on investments and servicing of finance	–
Investing activities	(58,000)
Payments to acquire fixed assets	(73,000)
Financing	100,000
Loan received	
Increase in cash and cash equivalents	£ 27,000

Figure 7.2 Book Selling Enterprises, Cash flow statement.

In this simple example, the cash flow statement is very close to the cash account which was drawn up in Figure 5.7 in Chapter 5.

❏ The direct and indirect method

The information provided in arriving at the net cash flow from operating activities has been calculated by the indirect method, i.e. reconciling from operating surplus by means of non-cash items.

The accounting standard, and the Treasury guidance, recommend that where possible the net cash flow should be calculated using the direct method, which states the different cash flows. According to the Accounting Standards Board:

the result is that reporting entities must give the information required by the indirect method, but may also give the information required by the direct method.

An example, from the National Physical Laboratory is given in Figure 7.3. below.

National Physical Laboratory
Cash flow statement

	£000	£000
Cash received from customers		50,713
Cash paid to suppliers	(20,519)	
Cash paid to and on behalf of employees	(17,898)	
Other cash receipts	663	
Running cost payments	(37,754)	
Superannuation paid	(2,766)	
		40,520
Net cash inflow from operating activities		£10,193

Figure 7.3 Cash flow statement National Physical Laboratory

This method provides more information than the indirect method but the information may be harder to produce. Organisations may therefore wish not to adopt it if they wish not to disclose more than is necessary. It is not compulsory, but the Accounting Standards Board say:

in those circumstances where the benefits to users of the information given by the direct method outweigh the costs of providing it the Board encourages reporting entities to provide the relevant information.

However, to enable comparisons with organisations using the indirect method, that information should also be given.

❑ Examples of cash flow statements

Figures 7.4 and 7.5b give two examples of cash flow statements, the examples again being the Ordnance Survey and Her Majesty's Stationery Office.

Interpreting the cash flow statement

The cash flow statement is intended to provide information on liquidity, viability and financial adaptability.

By examining each of the cash flow statements in Figures 7.4 and 7.5 in turn, the following pictures are revealed.

❏ Ordnance Survey

Ordnance Survey
Cash Flow Statement
for the Year Ended 31 March 1993

All amounts are in £ thousands

	Note	31 March 93	31 March 92
Net Cash Outflow from Operating Activities	6	(17 726)	(16 531)
Investing Activities			
Purchase of Tangible Fixed Assets	(4 003)		(2 255)
Receipts from sales of Tangible Fixed Assets	50		134
Net Cash Outflow from Investing Activities		(3 953)	(2 121)
Net Cash Outflow before Financing		(21 679)	(18 652)
Financing:			
Net vote expenditure appropriated in the year	7	20 004	18 099
Increase/(Decrease) in cash and cash			
equivalents	17	(1 675)	(553)

The notes on pages 21 to 28 form part of these Accounts

Figure 7.4 Cash flow statement Ordnance Survey.

The cash flow statement shows how an organisation making a deficit of £50m, as seen in Chapter 5, can suffer a cash reduction of only £2m. The main components of note 6 to the cash flow statement show that £24m of costs were a non-cash exceptional item. There were also £4m depreciation and £3m notional costs, also non cash items. £1m was released from working capital.

This then left Ordnance Survey with an £18m cash outflow from operating activities to fund, and a further £4m outflow for fixed assets. The vote provided £20m, leaving £2m to come from Ordnance Survey's own cash.

The future cash flows of Ordnance Survey are likely to be similar, with vote finance providing the money for the operating cash outflow and fixed asset purchases.

❏ HMSO

This cash flow shows that HMSO used the £12m cash from its operating activities to pay its net interest and buy £6m fixed assets. This left £6m, with which it has reduced its borrowings by £4m, and as a result cash has increased by £2m.

If HMSO continue to trade making a similar level of surplus and cash flow, it is likely that they will be able to repay all their loan borrowing and be self sufficient as far as cash is concerned, if the level of fixed asset purchases does not change significantly.

HMSO
Statement of Cash Flows

For the Year Ended 31 December 1993

	Notes	1993 £000	£000	1992 £000	£000
Net cash inflow from operating activities	4b		12,501		16,757
Servicing of finance					
Long-term interest paid		(1,145)		(1,703)	
Short-term interest paid		–		(317)	
Short-term interest received		1,616		1,486	
Finance lease interest		(173)		(250)	
Net cash outflow from servicing of finance			298		(784)
Investing activities					
Purchase of fixed assets		(6,637)		(3,231)	
Proceeds from sale of plant		305		607	
Net cash outflow from investing activities			(6,332)		(2,624)
Net cash inflow before financing			6,467		13,349
Financing					
New borrowings	18a	–		(5,000)	
Repayment of principal on finance lease	16b	1,004		685	
Repayment of borrowings	18c	3,339		18,939	
Net cash outflow from financing			4,343		14,624
(Decrease)/Increase in cash and cash equivalents	13		2,124		(1,275)
			6,467		13,349

Figure 7.5 Cash flow statement HMSO.

Cash flow forecast

The cash flow forecast is not part of the information found in a set of accounts. It is prepared by management to help them in forecasting the likely movements in cash, so that decisions can be taken about the level of bank balances or borrowing and the timing of discretionary payments, such as purchase of fixed assets.

This document is for internal purposes, and so there is no set format. In outline it may be:

	Period 1	Period 2	Period 3	etc
Receipts				
from trading	100	120	130	
other	10		20	
Payments				
to suppliers	(80)	(90)	(80)	
to staff	(20)	(20)	(30)	
other	(50)	(80)	(20)	
Net flow	(40)	(70)	20	
Opening Balance	200	160	90	
Closing Balance	160	90	110	

The cash flow forecast can be done for periods of a month, 4 weeks, 3 months or a year. The actual results should be compared against the plan each period and the remaining forecast revised.

References

Accounting Standards Board
Financial Reporting Standard 1
ASB, London   1991

H M Treasury 1991
Dear Accounting Officer letter GEN 16/91
Unpublished   1991

Chapter 8

Full published accounts

Agencies, trusts and quangos are all pumping out annual reports, business plans and performance charts but civil service mandarins, just like MPs, don't have any real idea about what to look for. (*John Garrett, 1993*)

The last three chapters have covered the basic elements in a set of commercial accounts, namely the operating account, the balance sheet and the cash flow statement. This chapter examines the requirements and guidance on all disclosures required.

Organisation	Operating account	Balance sheet	Cash flow statement
Fees and charges operation (note 1)	Yes	?	No
Government department (note 2)	?	?	?
Executive agency	Yes	Yes	Yes
Commercial operation	Yes	Yes	Yes
Non-departmental public body (note 3)	Yes	Yes	Yes
Nationalised industry	Yes	Yes	Yes
Public corporation	Yes	Yes	Yes
Health authority	Yes	Yes	Yes
NHS trust	Yes	Yes	Yes
Local authority	Yes	Yes	No
Charity	Yes	Yes	No
University	Yes	Yes	Yes
Housing association	Yes	Yes	Yes

Figure 8.1 Requirements of published accounts.
Notes:

1 A balance sheet is optional for a fees and charges operation, and often unavoidable if there are significant assets and liabilities.

2 Government departments. The exact form of the 'departmental resource accounts' is currently being developed. The consultation paper issued in July 1994 proposed an operating cost statement, a balance sheet and a cash flow statement.

3 Not all NDPBs have adopted commercial accounting. Those who have vary in what they have adopted. The table shows HM Treasury recommendations.

Figure 8.1 shows, for different types of public sector organisation, whether the three main documents, the operating account, the balance sheet and the cash flow statement, are required in a set of accounts.

The various types of public sector organisation are subject to different requirements concerning the presentation of their financial information, resulting in accounts with very different content and disclosures. These will be reviewed by looking at each part of the public sector in turn. Before that, however, the requirements with regard to accounting standards will be explained.

Accounting standards

Accounting standards are guidance documents issued to ensure maximum uniformity of treatment of accounting issues by different organisations. The standards are issued by the Accounting Standards Board (ASB), which is controlled by the Financial Reporting Council (FRC), an independent trust. (The standard setting process was run by the Accounting Standards Committee from 1969 until the creation of the ASB in 1990).

Although the standards do not in themselves have the force of law, the Companies Act 1989 introduced, into schedule 4 paragraph 36A of the Companies Act 1985, the requirement for large companies to state whether their accounts have been prepared in accordance with applicable accounting standards. Treasury rules do not allow public sector bodies to adopt the small companies' exemption from this. The Financial Reporting Review Panel, another part of the FRC, can also bring legal proceedings against companies whose accounts do not comply with the law. This might happen where a departure from the standards has resulted in the accounts not giving a true and fair view.

The foreword to the accounting standards says:

> The prescription of accounting requirements for the public sector in the United Kingdom is a matter for the Government. Where public sector bodies prepare annual reports and accounts on commercial lines, the Government's requirements may or may not refer specifically either to accounting standards or to the need for the financial statements concerned to give a true and fair view. However, it can be expected that the Government's requirements in such cases will normally accord with the principles underlying the Board's pronouncements, except where in the particular circumstance of the public sector bodies concerned the Government considers these principles to be inappropriate or considers others to be more appropriate.

There is a public sector committee which takes part in the standard setting process of the ASB and ensures that the standards developed are as relevant as possible to public sector bodies.

❏ The standards

At the time of writing, standards are in force covering the following areas:

Statements of standard accounting practice (SSAPs)

1	accounting for associated companies
2	disclosure of accounting policies
3	earnings per share
4	accounting for government grants
5	accounting for value added tax
8	the treatment of tax under the imputation system
9	stocks and long-term contracts
12	accounting for depreciation
13	accounting for research and development
15	accounting for deferred tax
17	accounting for post balance sheet events
18	accounting for contingencies
19	accounting for investment properties
20	foreign currency translation
21	accounting for leases and hire purchase contracts
22	accounting for goodwill
23	accounting for acquisitions and mergers
24	accounting for pension costs
25	segmental reporting.

Finantial reporting standards (FRSs)

1	cash flow statements
2	accounting for subsidiary undertakings
3	reporting financial performance
4	accounting for capital instruments
5	reporting the substance of transactions.

Some of these are of very limited relevance to the public sector. SSAPs 1, 22, 23 and FRS 2 relate to groups of organisations. A few of the nationalised industries, such as the Post Office, are concerned with them. SSAP 3 and FRS 4 relate to types of financing which are usually restricted to private sector companies. SSAPs

8 and 15 only affect organisations liable to Corporation tax. Again, in the public sector, this mainly affects nationalised industries. For those standards left, it must be emphasised that the detailed content will be found in the standards themselves, and explanation and interpretation in a book such as *'UK GAAP' (generally accepted accounting practice,)* (Ernst and Young 1992.) The following explanation is limited to the terms involved and the various accounting treatments possible.

- SSAP 2: Accounting policies; this covers accruals, prudence, consistency and going concern, and the need to disclose policies adopted

- SSAP 4: Government grants; grants to buy fixed assets are not to be netted off against the cost, but are to be shown on the balance sheet and written off over the life of the asset

- SSAP 5: VAT; turnover and all costs are net of VAT, unless it is irrecoverable

- SSAP 9: Stocks and long-term contracts; stocks are to be valued at the lower of cost and net realisable value. Long-term contracts may include a proportion of the surplus on the contract that has been earned by the balance sheet date

- SSAP 12: Depreciation; fixed assets are to be depreciated and the method and lives disclosed

- SSAP 13: Research and development; pure and applied research, including market research, is to be written off as it is incurred. Development expenditure can only be carried forward if it is on a clearly defined project, which is technically feasible and commercially viable, the costs are separately identifiable, the whole project will be profitable and resources exist to complete the project

- SSAP 17: Post balance sheet events; these are events occurring after the year end but before the accounts are published. They may be events which need to be disclosed simply for information the (e.g. the Minister is reviewing the future of the organisation,) or events which need the accounts to be adjusted (e.g. a major debtor has gone out of business, so the bad debt provision needs to be increased.) Many events will take place which are not material enough to require either adjustment or disclosure

- SSAP 18: Contingencies; these are contingent assets and liabilities, which do not need to be included in the accounts but do need to be disclosed for a full understanding. Examples are legal cases outstanding, or investments with a market value much higher than cost

- SSAP 19: Investment properties; these are properties which are wholly held for rental or capital growth, and are not occupied by the organisation. Such properties are not depreciated, but are included at open market value, which will fluctuate

- SSAP 20: Foreign currency translation; transactions and balances may be translated in the accounts at the historic rate, the average rate, the closing rate or a forward contract rate! This SSAP needs careful reading to see when each rate should be used

- SSAP 21: Leases and hire purchase contracts; the aim of this SSAP is to follow the principle of substance over form and treat fixed assets bought under HP or finance leases as belonging to the organisation from the outset. Operating leases are treated as rentals

- SSAP 24: Pension costs; this explains how to calculate the pension cost for defined contribution and defined benefit schemes.

- SSAP 25: Segmental reporting; turnover, surplus or deficit and net assets are to be disclosed by class of business and geographical segment

- FRS 1: Cash flow statements; these are to be prepared as set out earlier in Chapter 7

- FRS 3: Reporting financial performance; the results are to be split between continuing operations, acquisitions and discontinued operations, as shown in Chapter 5. A statement of total recognised gains and losses is required, as shown in Chapter 6

- FRS 5 : Reporting the substance of transactions; this requires the underlying commercial substance of all transactions to be presented in the accounts, thus reducing 'off - balance sheet' items.

❑ Urgent issues task force abstracts

Another step in the standard setting process is the issue by the Urgent Issues Task Force (UITF), another part of the FRC, of its abstracts. The aim is to act quickly to prevent misleading accounts and avoid the delay of up to three years that can occur while a standard is being issued. During this time a questionable practice might be widely imitated, and thus become 'generally accepted accounting practice', which would be harder to eliminate.

Abstracts currently in force are:

UITF3	Goodwill on disposal of a business
UITF4	Long-term debtors in current assets
UITF6	Post-retirement benefits other than pensions

UITF7   True and fair override

UITF9   Hyper-inflationary economies.

Of these, UITF4, UITF6 and UITF7 are the most likely to be significant for public sector bodies. They apply to all accounts intended to give a true and fair view, with immediate effect.

❏ Exposure drafts

In addition to accounting standards, exposure drafts are issued for discussion prior to the creation or amendment of a standard. At present there are:

Issued by the ASC

ED47   Goodwill

ED51   Fixed assets and revaluations

ED52   Intangible fixed assets

ED55   Investments

Issued by the ASB

\-   Objectives of financial statements and the qualitative characteristics of financial information

\-   Foreword to accounting standards

FRED2   Amendment to SSAP 15, accounting for deferred tax

FRED6   Acquisitions and mergers

FRED7   Fair values in acquisition accounting

\-   Goodwill and intangible assets

FRED8   Related party disclosures.

It is not necessary for any organisation to follow an exposure draft, but it may do so provided that this will not conflict with any accounting standard that is in force.

❏ Statements of recommended practice (SORPs)

The SSAPs, FRSs and UITFs apply to all accounts intended to give a true and fair view. SORPs, by contrast, are intended to apply to only one type of organisation. Relevant SORPs issued for the public sector by the ASC are:

SORP1   Pension scheme accounts

SORP2   Accounting by charities.

In addition to these SORPs issued by the ASC, individual bodies develop their own SORPs and get them 'franked' by the ASC and now the ASB. These are referred to in the later sections covering specific types of organisations.

Central Government

Central Government comprises government departments, fees and charges operations, executive agencies, trading funds and commercial operations. The differing reporting requirements are summarised in Figure 8.2.

Organisation	True and fair	Companies Act	SSAPs and FRSs	Extra disclosure
Government department–resource accounting	?	?	?	?
Fees and charges operations	No	No	No	Yes
Executive agencies and trading funds	Yes	Yes	Yes	Yes
Commercial operations	Yes	Yes	Yes	Yes

Figure 8.2 Reporting requirements in Central Government.

❏ Resource accounting

This is an area which is still being developed, and the proposals are that these accounts would be based on generally accepted accounting practice with extra disclosure especially in the area of achievement of objectives.

❏ Fees and charges operations

Operating accounts are prepared for all areas in departments where services are provided for a charge to other government departments or to the public. The prime purpose is to see whether prices properly reflect full cost. Many such service providers have become executive agencies. Those who are not executive agencies prepare forecast Memorandum Trading Accounts (MTAs), to assist in price setting, and after the year end, actual MTAs to see what actually happened. The rules for MTAs are contained in the Treasury *Fees and Charges Guide* (HM Treasury 1992), and in the *Costing Guide* (HM Treasury 1992).

The *Fees and Charges Guide* requires an operating account only.

> An MTA may be as simple or as sophisticated as its purpose requires, although it should normally be constructed on an accruals basis and there should be consistency in the accounting treatment of similar items within accounting periods and from one accounting period to the next.

National Weights and Measures Laboratory
Memorandum Trading account 1992–93

| | FEE EARNING ACTIVITIES | | | | | | Other Statutory and Policy Activities £ | TOTAL for all ACTIVITIES £ |
| | CALIBRATION AND TESTING | | | TYPE EXAMINATION | | | | |
	Calibration £	Equipment Testing £	All Testing £	Basic Patterns £	Variants £	All Patterns £		
INCOME								
Fees earned during year	93,777	127,388	221,165	145,297	123,228	268,525	86,237	575,927
Recoverable expenses	110	574	684	533	1,075	1,609	–	2,293
Less funds for 1992/93	–	–	–	–	3,194	3,194	10,306	13,500
Total Income	**93,887**	**127,962**	**221,849**	**145,830**	**121,109**	**266,939**	**75,932**	**564,720**
EXPENDITURE								
Staff cost	25,735	36,648	62,383	68,322	58,840	127,162	793,141	982,686
Staff accommodation	6,446	9,531	15,977	17,180	14,771	31,951	214,617	262,545
Laboratory accommodation	17,978	29,263	47,241	–	–	–	175,196	222,437
Administration	10,638	15,149	25,787	28,241	24,322	52,563	327,850	406,200
Common services	4,368	6,077	10,445	9,506	8,201	17,707	105,347	133,499
Office supplies	1,316	1,796	3,112	3,035	2,618	5,653	31,252	40,017
Materials/consumables	2,858	1,756	4,614	1,123	967	2,090	17,109	23,813
Miscellaneous services	1,601	2,370	3,971	4,250	3,661	7,911	143,035	154,917
Travel and subsistence	8,249	2,573	10,822	3,410	2,942	6,352	37,952	55,126
Depreciation and National Insurance	12,937	21,043	33,980	200	173	373	127,666	162,019
Interest on working capital	1,343	2,429	3,772	2,078	–	2,078	1,644	7,494
Total Expenditure	**93,468**	**128,635**	**222,103**	**137,346**	**116,495**	**253,841**	**1,974,810**	**2,450,754**
SURPLUS (DEFICIT)	**419**	**(673)**	**(254)**	**8,484**	**4,614**	**13,098**		

Figure 8.3 MTA for National Weights and Measures Laboratory.

However, there is a further requirement, which goes beyond a simple operating account:

> Where bodies provide more than one service a separate analysis, showing the financial objective, full cost, income, surplus/deficit and performance against the financial objective should be provided for each service in the notes to the account.

The MTA is not audited and does not need to be published, though one which is published is that for National Weights and Measures Laboratory. This is reproduced in Figure 8.3.

❏ Executive agencies and trading funds

Guidance on agency accounts is found in a number of sources. The most comprehensive starting point is the accounts direction for an individual agency. Once an executive agency is ready to progress from preparing an MTA to preparing auditable commercial accounts, an accounts direction is issued by the Treasury Officer of Accounts. It provides a clear indication of what the accounts are to include, and hence what will be audited. For on-vote agencies, the accounts direction is issued under Section 5 of the Exchequer and Audit Departments Act 1921. For trading funds, it is under Section 4(6) of the Government Trading Funds Act 1973.

An example of a typical accounts direction for an on-vote agency is that for the National Physical Laboratory. This is shown in Figure 8.4, and is taken from the Laboratory's 1992-93 Annual Report and Accounts.

This direction refers to a number of requirements, documents or standards which are now explained in more detail in the following sections. Immediately below there is some more information on the foreword, Government Accounting, the trading accounts booklet, a true and fair view, and the Companies Acts.

THE NATIONAL PHYSICAL LABORATORY

ACCOUNTS DIRECTION GIVEN BY THE TREASURY

The Treasury in pursuance of section 5 of the Exchequer and Audit Departments Act 1921, hereby gives the following direction:

1   The statement of accounts which it is the duty of the National Physical Laboratory to prepare in respect of the financial year ended 31 March 1992 and in respect of any subsequent financial year shall comprise:
- (a)   a foreword;
- (b)   an income and expenditure account;
- (c)   a balance sheet; and
- (d)   a cash flow statement,

including in each case such notes as may be necessary for the purposes referred to in the following paragraphs.

2   The National Physical Laboratory shall observe all relevant accounting and disclosure requirements given in *Government Accounting* and in the Treasury booklet *Trading Accounts: A Guide for Government Departments and Non–Departmental Public Bodies* (the 'Trading Accounts booklet') as amended or augmented from time to time.

3   The statement of accounts referred to above shall give a true and fair view of the income and expenditure, state of affairs and cash flows of the National Physical Laboratory.

     Subject to the foregoing requirement, the statement of accounts shall also, without limiting the information given and as described in Schedule 1 of this direction, meet:
- (a)   the accounting and disclosure requirements of the Companies Act;
- (b)   best commercial accounting practices including accounting standards issued or adopted by Accounting Standards Board; and
- (c)   any disclosure and accounting requirements which the Treasury may issue from time to time in respect of accounts which are required to give a true and fair view;

insofar as these are appropriate to the National Physical Laboratory and are in force for the financial period for which the statement of accounts is to be prepared.

4   Additional disclosure requirements are set out in Schedule 2 of this Direction.

5   The income and expenditure account and balance sheet shall be prepared under the historical cost convention modified by the inclusion of:
- (a)   fixed assets and their value to the business by reference to current costs; and
- (b)   stocks valued at the lower of cost, or net current replacement cost where materially different, and net realisable value.

Dated: 10 April 1992
Signed: J Beastall
           Treasury Officer of Accounts

SCHEDULE 1 ~ APPLICATION OF THE COMPANIES ACT'S REQUIREMENTS

1   The disclosure exemptions permitted by the Companies Act in force for the financial period for which the statement of accounts is to be prepared shall not apply to the National Physical Laboratory unless specifically approved by the Treasury.

2   The foreword shall contain the information required by the Companies Act to be disclosed in the Directors' Report, to the extent that such requirements are appropriate to the National Physical Laboratory.

3   In preparing its income and expenditure account and balance sheet, the National Physical Laboratory shall adopt the respective Format 1 prescribed in Schedule 4 to the Companies Act 1985 to the extent that such requirements are appropriate to the National Physical Laboratory. Regard should be had to the examples in Annex C of the Trading Accounts booklet, in particular the need to strike the balance sheet totals at 'Total Assets less Current Liabilities'.

4   The foreword and balance sheet shall be shall be signed and dated.

SCHEDULE 2 ~ ADDITIONAL DISCLOSURE REQUIREMENTS

1   The foreword shall state that the accounts have been prepared in accordance with a direction by the Treasury in the pursuance of section 5 of the Exchequer and Audit Departments Act 1921.

2   The foreword shall include a brief history of the National Physical Laboratory and its statutory background. Regard should be had to annexes B and C of the Trading Accounts booklet.

3   The notes to the accounts shall include details of the key corporate financial targets set by the Minister together with an indication of the performance achieved.

Figure 8.4 Accounts direction – National Physical Laboratory.

❏ Foreword

The content of the foreword is specified in Schedule 1, Section 2 and Schedule 2, Sections 1 and 2.

In practice, this content of the foreword will follow the guidelines in Annex C to the Treasury guidance on agency accounts (HM Treasury 1993) which are reproduced in Figure 8.5.

FOREWORD TO THE ACCOUNTS

The foreword should give information on the following matters:

    (a)   the principal activities of the organisation and any significant changes during the year,

    (b)   a review of development of the business and the position at year end,

    (c)   important events occurring after the year end,

    (d)   an indication of likely future developments,

    (e)   an indication of any activities in the field of research and development,

    (f)   significant changes in fixed assets held by the organisation,

    (g)   any material difference between the market value of interests in land held as fixed asset and its book value,

    (h)   any amount proposed to be paid as dividend and any amount retained and carried to reserves,

    (i)   the names of directors during the year. This will be interpreted as the Management Group or Board of Management, however described,

    (j)   details of charitable donations if these exceed £200 in aggregate,

    (k)   the policy in relation to disabled employees,*

    (l)   the action taken to maintain or develop the provision of information to, and consultation with, employees.*

    * (k) and (l) only apply if there are more than 250 employees in the UK.

Figure 8.5 Foreword to the accounts.

Government Accounting

The disclosure requirements in *Government Accounting* (Section 15.3, updated to *1994* wording) are as follows.

1 The accounts should be prepared on an accruals basis. They will comprise Foreword, Income and Expenditure Account, Balance Sheet, Cash Flow statement and Notes to the accounts, including a statement of accounting policies.

2 The notes to the accounts support the figures shown in the Income and Expenditure account and Balance Sheet and provide additional information which cannot be suitably displayed on the face of the principal statements.

3 Annual accounts should be as informative as possible, and accordingly no public sector body may take advantage of the exemption provisions of the Companies Acts which are available to small and medium-sized companies.

4 Unless positively inappropriate, the accounts should comply with the accounting provisions and disclosure requirements of the Companies Acts, SSAPs, FRSs and SORPs. These include the concepts of going concern, accruals, consistency and prudence.

5 The detailed accounting policies may be expected to cover the following items:

fixed assets and depreciation

leased assets

investments

stocks and work in progress

sales

borrowings

foreign currency transactions

research and development

insurance

interest on capital

grants

pensions

and any other relevant, significant or unusual items.

6 Unless the Treasury has advised otherwise, the accounts should be drawn up on a basis which reflects the effects of price changes on their operations.

7 Notional items should be included.

8 Financial targets, performance and explanation should be disclosed, taking into account any need for commercial confidentiality.

9 Bodies should consider including a year-in-brief summary, and a five year summary.

Trading accounts booklet

The *Trading Accounts* booklet refers to the requirements in *Government Accounting*, then adds the following:

1 the recommended formats for profit and loss accounts and balance sheets from the Companies Act

2 the content of the foreword

3 the balance sheet should be balanced at 'Total assets less current liabilities'

4 treatment of Government loan capital

5 treatment of grants

6 treatment of interest payable.

The largest part of the booklet is Annex C which contains a proforma set of accounts, on a historical cost basis.

True and fair view

This is the peg on which the Companies Act, accounting standards and Treasury requirements can be hung. It was discussed in Chapter 3.

Companies Acts

At present, there are the Companies Acts 1985 and 1989. Some key points from the Companies Act 1985, Schedule 4, are shown in Figure 8.6.

Companies Act 1985

Accounting Principles

10   The company shall be presumed to be carrying on business as a going concern.

11   Accounting policies shall be applied consistently from one financial year to the next.

12   The amount of any item shall be determined on a prudent basis, and in particular–
         (a)   only profits realised at the balance sheet date shall be included in the profit and loss account; and
         (b)   all liabilities and losses which have arisen or are likely to arise in respect of the financial year to which the accounts relate or a previous financial year shall be taken into account, including those which only become apparent between the balance sheet date and the date on which it is signed on behalf of the board of directors in pursuance of section 238 of this Act.

13   All income and charges relating to the financial year to which the accounts relate shall be taken into account, without regard to the date of receipt or payment.

Figure 8.6 Extract from the Companies Act 1985.

In addition, section 14, shown in Figure 8.7, states

Companies Act 1985

Extract From Schedule 4

14   In determining the aggregate amount of any item the amount of each individual asset or liability that falls to be taken into account shall be determined separately.

Figure 8.7 Section 14, Schedule 4, from the Companies Act 1985.

This prevents netting off of items, such as money owed to and by the same customer/supplier, or netting off a grant against a fixed asset purchased.

The content of the foreword, discussed above, is based on the Directors' Report requirements in Schedule 7 and Section 235 of the Act.

The formats of the operating accounts and balance sheets are in Sch 4 of the Act. The operating accounts recommended by HM Treasury are format 1, which classifies expense by function, as in cost of sales, and format 2 which classifies by type, as in salaries. The balance sheet format specified is the vertical one already explained in Chapter 6. The Act does permit 'horizontal' operating accounts and balance sheets.

Although the Companies Act is very specific about the words to be used on the accounts, *Trading Accounts* recognises that alternative words may be needed to arrive at something more meaningful for a public sector organisation.

Agency accounts

In addition to the guidance issued by accountancy bodies the Treasury has issued a working draft of guidance on agency annual reports and accounts. It covers a number of additional areas, such as the treatment of Consolidated Fund Extra Receipts for on-vote agencies, and it clearly distinguishes mandatory requirements from optional suggestions.

There is an annual Price Waterhouse competition and award for the best agency report and accounts. The award, made for clarity and technical excellence, was won in 1992 by the National Physical Laboratory, and in 1993 by Companies House.

Extracts from the accounts of Ordnance Survey, an on-vote agency, and HMSO, a trading fund, were given in Chapters 5, 6 and 7.

❏ Commercial operations

The organisations in this group, Crown Estate, Export Credit Guarantee Department (ECGD) and Forestry Commission, have all produced commercial accounts for a number of years. They are subject to the requirements shown in Figure 8.8.

Organisation	Cos Act	SSAPs FRS	Other requirements
Crown Estate	Yes	Yes	Crown Estate Act 1961
ECGD	Yes	Yes	Stock Exchange Listing Rules
Forestry Enterprise	Yes	Yes	The expectation value concept

Figure 8.8 Public sector commercial operations: accounting requirements.

The Crown Estate Act 1961 specifies that the accounts must distinguish between capital and revenue. When the Crown Estate grants a long lease on one of its properties, the tenant will often pay a lease premium. A lease premium received for a lease of a term of 30 years or less is treated as revenue, whereas it is capital if the lease is for over 30 years.

The Stock Exchange Listing Rules impose additional disclosure requirements on companies listed on the Stock Exchange. Although ECGD is not listed, it has to follow these requirements. Among the 19 detailed requirements, many concerning shares and directors, the following are the most relevant to public sector organisations:

- a commentary on forecast, providing an explanation if results are more than 10% different from forecast
- borrowings are to be shown as amounts due under 1 year, 1-2 years, 2-5 years and over 5 years
- names and biographies of non-executive directors
- a statement on compliance with the 'Code of Best Practice' of the Committee on the Financial Aspects of Corporate Governance - the 'Cadbury report.'

The Cadbury report requires listed companies, and encourages other companies, to:

- have clear division of responsibilities between a Chairman and a Chief Executive
- have strong, independent non-executive directors
- refer key matters for full board decision
- have an audit committee of non-executives which should appoint the auditors
- ensure that the directors report on internal controls
- ensure that the directors report whether the organisation is a going concern
- set up a remuneration committee to set board pay and bonuses.

The expectation value concept adopted by the Forestry Commission means that a proportion of the increase in the value of plantations is included each year, even though it may be decades before the trees are harvested.

❑ Non-departmental public bodies (NDPBs)

Although the Treasury booklet *Trading Accounts* is applicable to NDPBs, in practice the take up of accruals accounting is very patchy. For example, a comparison of two similar sized organisations illustrates how approaches differ.

The Arts Council is funded by grant-in-aid from the Department of National Heritage. Its accounts, on an accruals basis,

> are prepared under the historical cost convention. The accounts meet the requirements of the Companies Acts, and of the Statements of Standard Accounting Practice issued and adopted by the Accounting Standards Board, so far as those requirements are appropriate.

The total income of the Arts Council was £222m in 1992/93.

By comparison, the Medical Research Council, sponsored by the Office of Science and Technology, prepares accounts on a cash basis. These are prepared in accordance with a direction under the Science and Technology Act 1965. The accounts comprise a receipts and payments account, a statement of cash and bank balances and notes. The total operating receipts of the MRC were £226m in 1992/93.

As with executive agencies, once an NDPB is ready to have its accruals accounts audited, an accounts direction or financial memorandum is issued. This comes from the sponsoring department, rather than from the Treasury.

The accounts will then follow a common format:

- foreword
- income and expenditure account
- balance sheet
- cash flow statement
- notes to the accounts.

Some NDPBs are limited companies such as Remploy Limited, sponsored by the Employment Department. Others are registered charities such as the British Council, funded by the Foreign and Commonwealth Office. Charity requirements are discussed below. Such extra perspectives may bring differing and sometimes conflicting disclosure requirements.

❏ Nationalised industries

The main characteristic of this group is that they are expected, within the inevitable constraints of their public sector ownership and the boundary this imposes on their activities, to act commercially. As commercial undertakings they are liable to corporation tax on their taxable profits. Some freedoms are permitted in the way they structure their activities. This may result in groups of companies.

Most nationalised industries are statutory corporations, incorporated under specific Act of Parliament. The relevant legislation will specify that the accounts are to be drawn up in a form directed by the Secretary of State of the sponsor department. The remaining industries are simply incorporated under the Companies Act and therefore expected to observe the normal accounts requirements of that Act. In practice however there is little distinction, as the directions for the statutory corporations state that the requirements of the Companies Act and relevant accounting standards should be followed. A review of a few such industries illustrates what is required:

Organisation	Legislation	Cos Act SSAPs FRSs	Stock Exchange requirements	Other requirements
British Rail	Transport Act 1962	Yes	Yes	HC & MHC,detail
British Coal	Coal Industry Nationalisation Act 1946 and Coal Industry Act 1961	Yes	Yes	HC & CC,detail
Civil Aviation Authority	Civil Aviation Act 1982	Yes	Yes	HC & CC,detail
Post Office	British Telecommunications Act 1981	Yes	Yes	MHC,detail
London Transport	London Regional Transport Act 1984	Yes	Yes	MHC,detail

Fig 8.9. ~ Nationalised industries accounting requirements.

The nationalised industries are required to comply with the accounts disclosure requirements of the new Stock Exchange Listing Rules, insofar as they are appropriate. The Treasury has also encouraged industries to adopt voluntarily the Cadbury Code of corporate governance, and to reflect in annual reports the principles of the Operating and Financial Review published by the Accounting Standards Board.

The form of cost accounting used varies from historical cost (HC), modified historical cost (MHC) to current cost (CC). All have, in some way, to show the effect of price changes.

The annual reports of nationalised industries do not look dissimilar from equivalent-sized 'PLCs' in the private sector, except that in the interests of public accountability more detailed disclosure of the entities' activities and performance is provided. For example:

- British Rail has to provide segmental information for Inter City, Network South East, Regional Railways etc
- British Coal has to show social costs (redundancy, early retirement and retraining) separately
- the Post Office has to show quality of first and second class letter delivery, by postcode area.

Finally, as for making accounts more accessible, it is interesting to note that British Rail issued a summary of its accounts for 1987-88 on video for staff.

❏ Public corporations

Public corporations are basically similar to nationalised industries, except they are not actually classed as industries. Figure 8.10 shows the accounting requirements for a small number of such bodies.

Corporation	Cos Act	SSAPs FRSs	Cost	Other requirements
BBC	Yes	Yes	HC & part revaluation	Broadcasting Act 1990
S4C	Yes	Yes	HC	Details on Authority members
Bank of England	Yes	Yes	HC & part revaluation	Banking provisions
ITC	Yes	Yes	HC	Broadcasting Act 1990

Figure 8.10 Public corporations: accounting requirements

Here there is greater reliance on historical cost than was the case for the nationalised industries. The BBC only revalues its plant and machinery, and the Bank of England revalues property only.

The Bank of England accounts are for the banking department only, and they present a 'horizontal' balance sheet, with capital, reserves and current liabilities on the left side, and fixed and current assets on the right.

❏ Health authorities

The guidance for accounts for health authorities comes from the accounts directions which are drawn up by the relevant Secretary of State (for Health, Scotland or Wales) and approved by the Treasury. Health authorities are guided by standing financial instructions drawn up by the NHS Management Executive.

There is no requirement to publish annual accounts. The District Health Authorities (DHAs) usually only report internally to the Regional Health Authorities and to the Department of Health.

The Department of Health then publishes a summarised set of accounts. Those for 1991-92 were published in November 1993. They are prepared under a summarised accounts direction issued by the Treasury.

The components of the health authority accounts are:

- an income and expenditure account
- a balance sheet

- a cash flow statement
- notes to the accounts.

The income part of the income and expenditure account includes the money received from the Department of Health (Welsh Office, Scottish Office,) on the basis of cash received, not earned.

The threshold for capitalisation as a fixed asset is set at £5,000. There are particular rules on valuation of fixed assets and standard lives for depreciation purposes.

These are:

	Years
• vehicles	7
• mainframe IT	8
• furniture	10
• engineering installations	5, 10 or 15
• main structures	up to 80

This is in contrast to practice elsewhere, where individual organisations are free to select the lives that suit their circumstances.

Once the depreciation charge has been calculated, an interest charge, at 6% in real terms on the net book value of all fixed assets including land, is added to make the total capital charge.

A current liability which has to be identified separately is patients' money held by the authority, i.e. cash belonging to patients held by the authority during their stay in hospital.

The bottom half of the balance sheet is made up of three parts:

- capital account - the value of fixed assets bought with NHS funds
- donation reserve - the value of post 1948 donated assets
- balance due to or from the Department of Health - the balancing figure, which arises because all the other funds ultimately came from it.

❏ NHS trusts

An NHS trust is an organisation which operates in a similar way to a trading fund in central government, or a public corporation. It receives no direct funding from the Department of Health, and must win all its income by providing services to health authorities.

The accounts are governed by the National Health Service Act 1977, and will follow an accounts direction issued by the Department of Health with the approval of the Treasury. They comply with accounting standards as far as these are appropriate to NHS trusts.

The accounts comprise the same elements as health authorities:

- income and expenditure account
- balance sheet
- cash flow statement
- notes to the accounts.

The balance sheet distinguishes between fixed assets which have been purchased, and those donated. The value of donated assets is matched by a donation reserve, needed to make the balance sheet balance. The same fixed asset lives are specified as for health authorities. The bottom half of the balance sheet is made up as:

- Public Dividend Capital
- long-term loans
- revaluation reserve
- donation reserve
- other reserve
- income and expenditure account.

A trust is also obliged to report on its performance against its financial targets, as set by the NHS Management Executive, and include a note on clinical negligence costs.

A set of summarised accounts is produced for all the trusts, under an accounts direction issued by the Treasury.

❏ Family health service authorities

Up to 1992/93 family health service authorities prepared cash accounts. They now prepare accounts on the following format:

- an income and expenditure account
- a balance sheet
- a cash flow statement
- notes to accounts.

The form of accounts is prescribed in an accounts direction issued by the Secretary of State with the approval of the Treasury. Summarised accounts are published under an accounts direction issued by the Treasury.

❑ Local authorities

The formal accounting requirements originate from different legislation depending on whether the local authority is in England and Wales or in Scotland.

England and Wales

The requirements stem from the Local Government Finance Act 1982, and the Accounts and Audit Regulations 1983 as amended.

The regulations state that the accounts must include:

*   summarised income and expenditure account for each fund and undertaking
*   statement of capital expenditure
*   consolidated balance sheet
*   balance sheet for any funds not consolidated
*   statement of sources and applications of funds (the predecessor to the cash flow statement).

Guidance on the content of the annual report is contained in the Department of the Environment Code of Practice *Local Authority Annual Reports*. It recommends providing certain key statistics and indicators, which, together with the accounts, should help to inform Council Tax payers, electors and councillors.

The up-to-date requirements are contained in the CIPFA code of practice (see below.)

Scotland

The requirements in Scotland come from the Local Government (Scotland) Act 1973, and the Local Authority Accounts (Scotland) Regulations 1985. Scottish Office Finance Circular 5/1985 states that the Local Authority Scotland Accounts Advisory Committee (LASAAC) recommendations should be followed. LASAAC states that Scottish authorities should follow the CIPFA Code of Practice on Local Authority Accounting in Great Britain.

Code of Practice

The Code of Practice was first issued in 1987 by CIPFA and the Audit Commission, and it was revised in 1991 and 1993. It sets out the proper accounting practices required for accounts to comply with the Accounts and Audit regulations. It applies to local authorities, police and fire authorities, residuary bodies in England and Wales, and water development and river purification boards in Scotland. It does not apply formally to parish, town or community councils.

The Code of Practice states the accounting concepts that apply. The overriding requirement is to present fairly the financial position and results of operations, which is similar to giving a true and fair view. However, the term is used partly because not all SSAPs and FRSs, which must apply to all true and fair accounts, are appropriate.

The other concepts are matching, prudence, consistency, substance over form and materiality. Substance over form particularly applies to off balance sheet items.

The accounts are required to comprise:

- foreword
- accounting policies
- accounting statements
- notes.

The **foreword** has a very different content to that in central government accounts. It is to provide a concise explanation of the accounting statements, service expenditure and capital financing costs, material assets acquired or liabilities incurred, unusual charges or credits, changes in accounting policies, major changes in statutory functions and borrowings.

The 1993 Code of Practice gives guidance on accounting policies. Particular accounting policies which vary from those covered so far are as follows.

- Fixed assets are capitalised only if they have a life of 2 or more years, and only if they have been financed by borrowing. Finance lease assets are excluded. As a result, depreciation on all fixed assets is replaced by a capital charge, based on the debt which is financing some of the assets. Fixed assets appear in the balance sheet at the net amount of loans outstanding. Fixed assets financed from revenue or capital reserves do not necessarily appear in the balance sheet

- Deferred charges are included on the balance sheet, where expenditure has been made, there is no tangible fixed asset but there is still future benefit. Examples include road repairs, improvement grants and reorganisation costs

- The accounts are prepared on the historical cost basis, though current cost information can be provided.

The impact of the first of these can be seen in the accounts of Surrey County Council, whose balance sheet shows £183m of fixed assets. The notes indicate, however that fixed assets excluding land are actually insured for £1,500m! The fixed asset note is shown in Figure 8.11.

Surrey County Council
Fixed Assets Note

The council's fixed assets principally include........

	Holdings at 31 March 1993
Freehold land	4,085 Hectares
Leasehold land	76 Hectares
Freehold land associated with buildings	2,005 Hectares
Leasehold land associated with buildings	13 Hectares
County Hall	1
Other office buildings	95
First and Middle schools	368
*Secondary schools and sixth form colleges	47
Special schools and centres	30
* Further education colleges	6
Adult education centres	27
Staff development centres	5
Libraries	63 (incl 12 mobile)
Fire Brigade HQ and Training School	1
Fire stations	24
Fire vehicles	163
County Supplies HQ and warehouse	1
Highway and Transport depots	9
Transport fleet vehicles and plant	1,976
Principal roads	736 Kilometres
Other roads	3,971 Kilometres
Waste Disposal sites	15
Magistrates' Court Houses	11
Surrey Police HQ and Training School	1
Police stations and offices	38
Traffic Centres and motorway control team	4
Police houses	452
Police vehicles	365
Social Services residential homes	55
Social Services day care centres	22
Gypsy caravan sites	18

* Note:–

Under the provision of the Further and Higher Education Act 1992, six FE Colleges and seven Sixth Form Colleges will be independent of the County Council from 1 April 1993.

Figure 8.11 Fixed asset note from Surrey County Council accounts.

This note is very informative, listing the actual assets themselves. These disclosures are higher than the norm in the rest of the public sector.

A new capital accounting system for 1994/95 will radically change the approach adopted on capitalisation and cost method.

The **accounting statements** are:

- summary revenue account (general or county fund)
- housing revenue account
- collection fund (England & Wales)
- consolidated balance sheet
- statement of revenue and capital movements
- summary direct service organisation (DSO) revenue and appropriation accounts
- superannuation fund income and expenditure account and net assets statement
- in Scotland, for water and sewage, a separate summary revenue account.

On the following pages Figures 8.12, 8.13 and 8.14, taken from the Surrey County Council accounts, respectively illustrate the summary revenue account, consolidated balance sheet, and consolidated statement of revenue and capital movements.

Direct service organisation (DSO) accounts have been required to be prepared on an accruals basis since 1980.

Surrey County Council
Summary Revenue Account

Note	On its services other than Police the Council spent............	1992/93 Gross Expenditure £000	1992/93 Income £000	1992/93 **Net Expenditure** £000	1991/92 Net Expenditure £000
	Education				
1	Schools	304,049	31,208	**272,841**	258,159
1	Continuing Education	136,773	95,293	**41,480**	43,688
	Other Education	33,301	4,905	**28,396**	28,710
	Fire and Consumer Protection				
	Fire	25,264	532	**24,732**	23,381
	Trading Standards	2,520	140	**2,380**	2,155
	Libraries Leisure and Countryside				
	Libraries and Leisure				
	Countryside	16,104	1,099	**15,005**	12,191
	Registration of Births, Deaths & Marriages	2,349	310	**2,039**	2,034
	Commons Registration	965	298	**667**	561
		72	14	**58**	53
	Highways and Transport				
	Highways	94,766	39,609	**55,157**	51,462
	Transportation Planning & Programming	9,661	891	**8,770**	7,900
	Waste Management	8,502	565	**7,937**	7,307
	Magistrates Courts	5,766	4,626	**1,140**	1,207
	Planning	4,270	1,281	**2,989**	2,667
	Probation	5,723	4,605	**1,118**	956
	Social Services	87,345	12,162	**75,183**	63,849
	Other Services				
	Rent Officer	312	312	**0**	0
	Coroner	645	0	**645**	652
	Gipsy Caravan Sites	444	0	**444**	418
	Emergency Planning	412	395	**17**	19
	Corporate Expenses	7,582	0	**7,582**	6,947
	Compensation and Redundancy	1,273	0	**1,273**	1,425
	Valuers Property Services	2,917	1,939	**978**	1,465
	Village Halls/Community Centres	126	0	**126**	124
	giving total expenditure on services other than Police of......	751,141	200,184	**550,957**	517,330

Figure 8.12 Summary revenue account: Surrey County Council.

Surrey County Council
Summary Revenue Account (continued)

Note	Other income and expenditure included.............	1992/93 Gross Expenditure £000	1992/93 Income £000	1992/93 Net Expenditure £000	1991/92 Net Expenditure £000
	Land Drainage Precept	4,001	0	**4,001**	3,973
3	Write–off of Expenditure	65	0	**65**	18
4	Contributions from Trading Undertakings	0	1,950	**(1,950)**	(2,366)
5	Asset Rents Accounts Surplus	6,347	11,283	**(4,936)**	(1,978)
	Interest on Internal Balances	0	12,274	**(12,274)**	(11,862)
6	Reduction in Capital Financing Repayments	(11,995)	0	**(11,995)**	(13,460)
7	Residual Precept Repayments	966	0	**966**	1,406
6	Reduced Revenue Contribution to Capital	(4,557)	0	**(4,557)**	(17,842)
8	Contribution to Insurance Fund	1,000	0	**1,000**	0
9	Contribution to Capital Financing Reserve	11,666	0	**11,666**	24,392
10	Contribution to Investment and Renewal Reserve	234	0	**234**	0
	Provision for bad debts and losses	400	0	**400**	0
	Government Grant for Teachers pay award	0	994	**(994)**	0
	Boundary adjustment with Berkshire	0	0	**0**	520
11	Provision for loss of Part III Income	0	0	**0**	500
	giving total other income and expenditure of...	8,127	26,501	**(18,374)**	(16,699)
	Total Net expenditure was...	759,268	226,685	**532,583**	500,631
	This was financed by.......... Precept income	0	540,233	**(540,233)**	(501,217)
	to produce a surplus for the year of...	759,268	766,918	**(7,650)**	(586)
	General County balances at the start of the year were...			**(15,147)**	(14,561)
	Leaving year end balances of...			**(22,797)**	(15,147)
	On the Police service the Council spent...	75,212	39,392	**35,820**	32,214
	It received... Precept income	0	35,365	**(35,365)**	(32,423)
	Interest on Internal Balances	0	531	**(531)**	(694)
	Residual Precept Repayments	109	0	**109**	59
	These produce a deficit/(surplus) for the year of...	75,321	75,288	**33**	(844)
	Police balances at the start of the year were...			**(2,147)**	(1,303)
	Leaving year end balances of...			**(2,114)**	(2,147)

Figure 8.12 Summary revenue account: Surrey County Council.

Surrey County Council
Consolidated Balance Sheet

Note	The County Council has net fixed assets on which debt outstanding is...	£000	As at 31.3.93 £000	As at 31.3.92 £000
1	– land and buildings	123,439		
1	– infrastructure	51,561		
1	– equipment	7,791		
			182,791	165,141
3	**deferred charges of...**		3,739	2,255
4	**investments which cost...**		493	458
5	**and loans to be repaid to it of...**		3,131	3,406
	giving total long term assets of...		190,154	171,260
	The County Council's current assets are...			
	– stocks and work–in–progress	3,081		3,150
	– payments in advance	2,691		2,283
6	– debts due to it	43,706		39,589
7	– temporary loan investments	39,600		21,250
7	– cash with accounting officers	8,731		1,044
9	**these are offset by current liabilities of...**		97,809	
	– amounts received in advance	(1,160)		(935)
	– short term creditors	(75,882)		(61,126)
8	– cash overdrawn	(14,342)		(13,360)
			(91,384)	
	giving net current assets/liabilities (–) of...		6,425	(8,105)
	Total net assets are therefore...		196,579	(163,155)

Note	The County Council finances this from...	£000	As at 31.3.93 £000	As at 31.3.92 £000
10	– Long term borrowing		**69,472**	59,874
11	– Balances held on behalf of third parties		**1,953**	1,413
12	– Unused Capital Receipts		**39,465**	36,940
	Provisions			
13	– Vehicle Replacement Fund		**9,234**	8,641
13	– Equipment Replacement Fund		**438**	290
13	– Insurance Fund		**2,161**	0
13	– Part III Accommodation		**2,000**	2,000
13	– LMS Renewals Fund		**5,508**	7,009
13	– Direct Service Organisations		**626**	643
	Reserves			
14	– Investment and Renewal Reserve		**4,400**	4,659
14	– Revenue Surplus			
14	– General Reserve	18,733		13,667
14	– Capital Financing Reserve	36,411		24,392
14	– Schools and FE Colleges	6,178		3,627
			61,322	
			196,579	163,155

Figure 8.13 Consolidated balance sheet: Surrey County Council.

Surrey County Council
Consolidated Statement of Revenue and Capital Movements

	1992/93		1991/92	
	£000	£000	£000	£000
Revenue expenditure was...				
Employment costs	474,342		441,312	
Other operating costs	286,330		236,341	
Interest and lease payments	33,729		32,770	
		794,401		710,423
Capital expenditure was...				
Fixed assets	69,630		58,320	
Deferred charges	1,565		1,799	
Investments	35		33	
		71,230		60,152
Giving total revenue and capital expenditure of...		865,631		770,575
Revenue income was..				
Government grants	112,632		93,686	
Charges for services	144,752		113,405	
Precept	575,598		533,640	
Other income	14,108		13,263	
		847,090		753,994
Capital income was..				
Sale of assets	10,927		17,477	
Capital grants	10,459		8,558	
Other income	1,547		1,439	
		22,933		27,474
Giving total revenue and capital income of...		870,023		781,468
The difference between expenditure and income was		(4,392)		(10,893)
This was accounted for by...				
Net new long term borrowing	(9,598)		(14,345)	
Change in short term borrowing/lending	25,055		27,123	
		15,457		12,778
And changes in other short term assets/liabilities of..				
Increased(-) /reduced creditors	(15,521)		(2,947)	
Increased/reduced(-) debtors	4,525		837	
Increased/reduced(-) stock & work-in-progress	(69)		225	
		(11,065)		(1,885)
		4,392		10,893

Figure 8.14 Statement of revenue and capital movements: Surrey County Council.

❏ Charities

There are two different sources of control over the accounts of charities, namely the Charities Act and the Statement of Recommended Practice. All charities are governed by the Charities Act 1993. This states that all charities are to produce accounts.

There are four categories of charities and their accounting requirements are different:

- exempt charities are to prepare income and expenditure accounts and balance sheets
- registered charities with income of less than £25,000 may prepare a receipts and payments account (i.e. cash) and a statement of assets and liabilities
- larger registered charities have to prepare accounts in line with regulations, which have not yet been issued
- charities which are companies have to comply with the Companies Act.

SORP 2, *Accounting for Charities* was issued in 1988, and a revised version was issued as an exposure draft in 1993. The revised SORP may be issued in late 1994.

In practice, this means that larger charities which are not companies are at present only bound by the requirements of the Charities Act 1960, with the 1988 SORP regarded as best practice. The Charities Act 1960 only requires accounts to be prepared, but nothing prevents them from following the presentation format of revised SORP2 as issued in the 1993 exposure draft.

Public sector charities include many such as the British Museum, National Gallery, Tate Gallery, National Portrait Gallery, Wallace Collection and the National Curriculum Council, which all fall within the exempt category. Others in the public sector include the British Council, the largest charity in the United Kingdom, and the Arts Council, which are large registered charities.

Public sector charities will be pulled in two ways. They will be required to follow the Charities Act and the SORP. However, if the charity is an NDPB, then it will be governed by a financial memorandum from the main sponsoring department, which may ask for accruals based accounts following the *Trading Accounts* booklet. This can cause conflict where the charity does not wish to break the Charities Act nor displease its funding department. An example is the requirements under SSAP 25 to provide segmental information, and under *The Fees and Charges Guide* to show results for different services. These may cut across the SORP guidance which only asks for expenditure to be split between direct charitable expenditure and other expenditure. A public sector charity may therefore have to disclose more than other organisations, such as non-public sector charities or private sector bodies who are competing for funds and business, and feel at a disadvantage.

❏ Universities and other educational establishments

Universities receive a significant amount of their funds from Government, from the Department for Education, Scottish Office or Welsh Office via the Higher Education Funding Councils.

There is a Statement of Recommended Accounting Practice in UK Universities, issued in 1989 by the Committee of Vice Chancellors and Principals of the UK Universities. This committee has since then widened its scope, to include 'new' universities and higher education colleges. A new SORP *Accounting for United Kingdom Higher Education* has been developed by the committee, and is currently awaiting franking by the ASB.

University accounts consist of:

- report
- accounting policies
- income and expenditure account
- statement of financial position (balance sheet)
- cash flow statement
- notes to the accounts.

In general, the accounts follow standard accounting practice. There are some areas where standard practice may not be as informative and University accounts diverge. Examples, from the University of St Andrews, include :

- expenditure on equipment and furniture is not capitalised
- restricted income and expenditure are separately identified (income and expenditure are restricted if they relate to funds granted for specific purposes)
- £75m of books and other valuable collections were not included on the balance sheet, which totalled £47m.

In addition, the Open University follows *The Fees and Charges Guide*. Many universities are charities, but are usually exempt from the accounting provisions of the Charities Act.

The Further and Higher Education Act 1992 established all further education and sixth form colleges as independent charitable trusts with corporate status. They are exempt charities under the Charities Act 1993, and so currently need only prepare income and expenditure accounts and balance sheets.

City technology colleges (CTCs) are set up as charitable companies limited by guarantee. They have to prepare their accounts in accordance with the Financial Reporting and Annual Accounts Requirements (part 3 of the *CTC Blue Book* guidance) issued by the Department for Education. This requires CTC accounts to contain:

- report of the Governors
- income and expenditure account

- balance sheet
- cash flow statement
- notes to the accounts.

Grant maintained schools are required to follow the information in the Financial Report and Annual Accounts Requirements section of the *Rainbow Pack,* and all subsequent financial circular letters.

The accounts follow all the principles of accruals accounting and accounting standards, except that all capital expenditure is written off immediately, and all capital grants are treated as income immediately.

Grant maintained school accounts contain:

- an income and expenditure account
- a statement of financial position
- a cash flow statement
- notes to the accounts (without disclosing accounting policies).

❏ Housing associations

Housing association accounts are governed by the Housing Associations Act 1985, the Housing Act 1988 and the Registered Housing Associations (Accounting Requirements) Order 1992. In addition, depending on their status, they may also be subject to the Companies Act, the Charities Act or the Friendly and Industrial and Provident Society Act.

The content of the accounts required by the 1992 Order is:

- an income and expenditure account
- a balance sheet
- notes to the accounts.

In addition, some housing associations produce cash flow statements. The Order states that the accounts need to follow the concepts of going concern, consistency, prudence and accruals, and to give a true and fair view. The income and expenditure account and the balance sheet are to follow the vertical formats set out in the Companies Act.

A particular analysis of the income and expenditure account is required. This is illustrated by the extract from the accounts of the Hanover Housing Association in Figure 8.15.

Compliance with, or departure from, accounting standards and statements of

HANOVER HOUSING ASSOCIATION

NOTES TO THE FINANCIAL STATEMENTS FOR THE YEAR ENDED 31 MARCH 1993

2) TURNOVER, OPERATING SURPLUS AND SURPLUS

	1992/93							1991/92		
	Turnover	Operating costs	Cost of sales	Operating surplus	Interest receivable	Interest payable	Surplus/ Deficit	Turnover	Operating surplus	Surplus/ Deficit
	£'000	£'000	£'000	£'000	£'000	£'000	£'000	£'000	£'000	£'000
Income and Expenditure from lettings										
Housing accommodation	16,950	(12,499)		4,451			1,361	15,001	3,625	477
Residential home	31	(256)		(225)			(225)	243	(236)	(236)
Shared ownership accommodation	135	(114)		21			21	126	36	36
	17,116	(12,869)		4,247		(3,090)	1,157	15,370	3,425	277
Other Income and Expenditure										
Managed associations	647	(874)		(227)			(227)	721	(14)	(14)
Developments for sale	6		(16)	(10)			(10)	119	157	157
Other	943	(1,470)		(527)			(527)	986	(72)	(72)
Total	18,712	(15,213)	(16)	3,483		(3,090)	393	17,196	3,496	348
Investment income					909		909			1,054
Interest payable						(6)	(6)			(13)
Surplus for year				3,483	909	(3,096)	1,296		3,496	1,389

	1992/93 £'000	1991/92 £'000
Turnover from lettings		
Rents and service charges	17,284	15,427
Losses from bad debts and voids	(315)	(207)
	16,969	15,220
Grants from local authorities and other agencies	53	55
Other income	94	95
	17,116	15,370
Operating costs		
Direct costs	14,331	13,136
Administrative costs	882	602
	15,213	13,738

Figure 8.15 Turnover, operating surplus and surplus: Hanover Housing Association.

HANOVER HOUSING ASSOCIATION

NOTES TO THE FINANCIAL STATEMENTS FOR THE YEAR ENDED 31 MARCH 1993

2) TURNOVER, OPERATING SURPLUS AND SURPLUS (continued)

Service Income, Housing Corporation Allowances and Other Operating costs

	1992/93						1991/92			
	Service income £'000	Housing Corporation Allowances £'000	Operating costs £'000	Surplus/(deficit) before transfers £'000	Transfers to designated reserves £'000	Surplus/(deficit) after transfers £'000	Service income £'000	Operating costs £'000	Surplus/(deficit) before transfers £'000	Transfers (to)/from designated reserves £'000
Housing accommodation 8,740 units (1992 8,428 units)										
Service income and allowance activities										
Services	4,863		(4,838)	25	(307)	(282)	4,268	(4,385)	(117)	(257)
Residential home	31		(256)	(225)		(225)	143	(479)		
Management		2,617	(2,833)	(216)		(216)		(2,433)	(38)	
Day to day repairs & maintenance		1,851	(1,711)	140		140		(1,621)	89	
Cyclical repairs & maintenance		1,567	(903)	664		664		(1,287)	481	
Total service charges and allowance activities	4,894	6,035	(10,541)	388	(307)	81	4,411	(10,205)	415	(257)
Other activities										
Programmed repairs			(1,978)	n/a				(1,456)	n/a	
Other			(236)	n/a				(66)	n/a	
Shared ownership			(114)	n/a				(90)	n/a	
			(12,869)					(11,817)		
Rent surplus fund					(943)			(128)		(625)
Major repairs provision					(602)					1,296
Other transfers (to)/from reserves					(1,852)					414
Housing accommodation			(12,499)					(11,376)		
Residential home			(256)					(479)		
Shared ownership			(114)					(90)		
			(12,869)					(11,945)		

Figure 8.15 Turnover, operating surplus and surplus: Hanover Housing Association (continued)

recommended practice (SSAPs, FRSs and SORPs) must be stated. In addition, information is required regarding directors, employees, auditors, fixed assets, investments, reserves, deferred tax, creditors, rent arrears, charges, debentures, loans, non-housing activities, special circumstances and subsidiary undertakings. In most cases, these disclosure requirements are similar to those for other organisations reporting under the Companies Act and accounting standards.

The SORP *Accounting by Registered Housing Associations*, issued in 1994, requires housing association accounts to move to a format closer to that followed by companies. This requires all associations to show their properties at historical cost, net of housing association grant, or at valuation.

Developments in accounting

Any organisation can consider disclosing extra information before it becomes a technical requirement. There are two areas being considered by the private sector which may have an effect on public sector accounts in the future. The areas are human asset accounting and environmental accounting.

❏ Human asset accounting

Accounting for people is particularly important in the public sector where often the cost of staff is more than half the total running costs. Human asset accounting reflects the fact that it may not be accurate to write off all staff costs in the year they are spent, but the worth of the organisation would be better reflected by including a valuation of the costs of training and developing staff in the balance sheet.

❏ Environmental accounting

Environmental accounting means accounting for the impact that the organisation has on the environment. Disclosure in the annual report and accounts might include the organisation's environmental policy and objectives, and the amount spent on them, what the impact of the organisation on the environment is, its compliance with regulations and any significant risks not provided for or disclosed as a contingent liability.

❏ Dates for publication

The year end for public sector organisations is usually 31 March, to coincide with the Treasury financial year.

Exceptions to this include HMSO and the Buying Agency, both trading funds, and S4C, all of whom have a 31 December year end.

British Coal draws up its accounts to the last Saturday in March, so that it has some 52 and some 53 week years.

Universities and colleges are likely to have a year end which reflects their academic year or funding year, 31 July or 31 August.

The deadline for **publication** of the accounts for each type of organisation is as follows:

Fees and charges operations	not published
Executive agencies	before summer recess of Parliament i.e. late July
Commercial operations	
Crown Estate	
Forestry Commission	to auditors by 30 November
ECGD	'as soon as practicable'
N D P Bs	various
Nationalised industries	6 months of the year end
Public corporations	various
Health authorities	30 June
NHS trusts	30 June
Local authorities	
England & Wales	prepare by 30 Sept, publish by 31 Dec
Scotland	prepare by 31 August
Charities	10 months
Universities	31 December
City technology colleges	31 December
Grant maintained schools	31 August
Housing associations	30 September

References

Accounting Standards Board
Foreword to Accounting Standards - Exposure draft
ASB, London   1991

CIPFA /LASAAC
Code of Practice on Local Authority Accounting in Great Britain
CIPFA, London   1993

CIPFA
The Application of Accounting Standards (SSAPs) to Local Authorities in Great Britain
CIPFA, London   1991

CIPFA
Introductory Guide to NHS Finance in the UK
CIPFA, London   1993

CIPFA
Local Authority Accounting Handbook
CIPFA, London   1993

Ernst & Young
UK GAAP (Generally Accepted Accounting Practice)
MacMillan, London   1992

Department of the Environment
Code of Practice 'Local Authority Annual Reports'
HMSO, London   1981

John Garrett
Public Finance
IPF Ltd, London   10 December 1993

HM Treasury
Costing Guide
Unpublished   1992

HM Treasury
The Fees and Charges Guide
HMSO, London   1992

HM Treasury
Government Accounting
HMSO, London   1989 as amended

HM Treasury
Trading Accounts: A Guide for Government Departments and Non-Departmental Public Bodies
HMSO, London   1989

London Stock Exchange
The Listing Rules
London Stock Exchange, London   1993

Chapter 9

Audit

An auditor is not bound to be a detective, or to approach his work with suspicion or with a foregone conclusion that there is something wrong. He is a watchdog, but not a bloodhound. *(Lopez, 1896)*

Audit work is carried out by internal or external auditors. This chapter describes the different work which they do, and describes the main features of the results of their work, concentrating on the work done in relationship to financial accounts.

Internal audit

Internal audit is an independent appraisal within a department which operates as a service to management by measuring and evaluating the effectiveness of the internal control system.

This statement is taken from the Government Internal Audit Manual (HM Treasury 1988). The objective of internal auditing is to help members of the organisation, at all levels, to discharge their responsibilities effectively. Most public sector organisations will be subject to internal audit.

Internal controls are established by management to:

- achieve organisational objectives
- ensure economical and efficient use of resources
- ensure compliance with established policies, procedures, laws and regulations
- safeguard the organisation's assets and interests from losses of all kinds, including those arising from fraud, irregularity and corruption
- control liabilities
- ensure the integrity and reliability of information and data.

The scope of internal audit is not limited to the controls over financial resources, but covers the whole range of systems of internal controls.

Internal auditors must be, and be recognised as, independent. This can be achieved in a number of ways:

- the internal audit department should report directly to senior management, at a high enough level to ensure that recommendations are not lost, and are followed through. Such reporting may be to an Audit Committee, which is itself independent of the organisation's senior management

- the staff should carry out their work freely and objectively. For example, they should not develop systems which they will later need to audit, although they can advise on the control needs and auditor requirements to those who are developing the systems.

As a result of their work, internal auditors provide :

- reviews of systems and recommendations on how controls can be improved in these systems
- advice on controls in developing systems
- assurance to the Accounting Officer / Principal Finance Officer on the reliance that can be placed on the organisation's systems of control.

It is possible that the staff involved in the internal audit work could be from outside the organisation. This may be achieved for an executive agency by the parent department's internal auditors conducting the internal audit of the agency. Independence may be achieved in other ways. The Royal Mint's internal audit is carried out by a firm of accountants, and an increasing number of internal audits are being market tested or contracted out. Internal audit consortia exist for local authorities, NHS bodies and universities, providing a service to more than one such organisation.

Internal audit will not seek to certify the accounts themselves, or otherwise draw an opinion on them. They may review the controls underlying the preparation of the accounts and the application of accounting conventions.

However independent the internal audit team is, it is carrying out a service for the organisation and its management. This does not give it sufficient independence to act as external auditors, who are reporting to all users of the accounts.

❑ External audit

External audit is the independent examination of, and expression of opinion on, the financial statements of an enterprise. The exposure draft, *Statement of Auditing Standards 100* (Auditing Practices Board 1993) includes the following.

> The responsibility for the preparation and presentation of the financial statements is that of the management of the entity. The auditors are responsible for forming

and expressing an opinion on the financial statements. The audit of the financial statements does not relieve management of its responsibilities.

If internal auditors have carried out work for the organisation, then the external auditors may be able to rely in part on that work.

In deciding whether they should do so, they will, according to the exposure draft of *Statement of Auditing Standard 500* (Auditing Practices Board, 1993), consider whether:

- the work is performed by persons having adequate technical training and proficiency as internal auditors
- the work of assistants is properly supervised, reviewed and documented
- sufficient appropriate audit evidence is obtained to afford a reasonable basis for the conclusions reached
- the conclusions reached are appropriate in the circumstances
- any reports prepared by internal audit are consistent with the results of the work performed
- any exceptions or unusual matters disclosed by internal audit are properly resolved
- amendments to the external audits programme are required as a result of matters identified by internal audit work, and
- there is a need to test the work of internal audit to confirm its adequacy.

Organisation	Auditor
Executive agency	National Audit Office
Commercial operation	National Audit Office
Non-departmental public body	National Audit Office/Accountancy firm
Nationalised industry	Accountancy firm
Public corporation	Accountancy firm
Health authority	
Family health authority	Audit Commission/Accountancy firm
NHS trust	
GP fundholder	
NHS summarised accounts	National Audit Office.
Local authority	Audit Commission/ Scottish Accounts Commission/Accountancy firm
Charity - large	Registered auditor - accountancy firm
- small	Independent examiner
University	Accountancy firm
Other educational establishment	Accountancy firm
Housing association	Accountancy firm

Figure 9.1 External auditors.

External audits are carried out on public sector organisations by different independent bodies, as shown in Figure 9.1.

The Memorandum Trading Account prepared by a fees and charges operation is not published or audited, though it is open to inspection by the NAO and can be referred to in its reports. Similarly, executive agencies produce unaudited accounts in their first few years.

We now look at these external auditors individually.

❑ National Audit Office

The National Audit Office (NAO) was set up in 1866 as a government department, the Exchequer and Audit Department. In 1983 it was reorganised and renamed, and the NAO is now independent of Government.

It is headed by the Comptroller and Auditor General (C&AG), who is an officer of the House of Commons, and the staff are not civil servants. The C&AG audits the accounts of all Government departments, including executive agencies, and also the accounts of a range of other public sector bodies.

The work carried out by the NAO falls into two groups, designed to show whether public money has been properly spent. Approximately half the work of the NAO's 800 staff is on the financial audit of some 500 statements each year. Some, including the main Appropriation Accounts, are prepared on a cash basis, and receive a 'properly presents' opinion. The remainder are prepared on an accruals basis and are subject to a 'true and fair' opinion. All are subject to the public sector requirement regarding regularity, propriety and compliance with authority. The remainder of the staff work on the 50 or so value for money audits each year. As well as the duty of auditing financial accounts, the C&AG has a statutory right to report to Parliament on the economy, efficiency and effectiveness with which departments and other bodies have used their resources. The final section of this chapter says a little more about these value for money audits.

The National Audit Office's own accounts are cash accounts, which are audited by an accountancy firm.

❑ Accountancy firms

To be eligible to carry out audits firms must be partnerships controlled by regulated auditors who may be either Chartered Accountants or Certified Accountants. The top 10 firms, ranked by total UK fee income from all sources in 1994 were, according to *Accountancy (1994)*

	Fees £m	Partners and staff
Coopers & Lybrand	560	6,942
KPMG Peat Marwick	498	6,773
Arthur Andersen	433	4,202
Ernst & Young	388	4,837
Price Waterhouse	385	4,334
Touche Ross	342	4,230
Grant Thornton	107	1,658
BDO Binder Hamlyn	107	1,707
Pannell Kerr Forster	80	1,487
Stoy Hayward	78	1,315

These firms may be involved in central government as consultants or internal auditors. In the rest of the public sector they may also act as external auditors, and in these circumstances they would ensure the appropriate division of responsibilities so that their independence as external auditors was not affected.

The accounts of accountancy firms are not audited or published because the firms are partnerships with unlimited liability.

❑ Audit Commission

The Audit Commission was established in 1983, and took over responsibility for the external audit of local authorities previously exercised by the Department of the Environment, the District Audit Service. In 1990 it took on the audit of those National Health Service accounts which were not audited by the NAO. These audits had previously been carried out by the Audit Directorate of the Department of Health and Social Security. It was then renamed the Audit Commission for Local Authorities and the National Health Service in England and Wales, and it is an executive NDPB.

There are about 450 audits of local authorities and 600 of health organisations. These are statutory audits which include reviews of economy, efficiency and effectiveness as well as the expression of an opinion on the financial statements. In practice, the Audit Commission awards about 30% of these audits to eight of the accountancy firms, and the remainder are carried out by its directly employed arm, the District Audit Service. There are some 140 headquarters staff, and 1,000 in the District Audit Service.

In the National Health Service, the Audit Commission is responsible for the audit of health authorities, family health service authorities, NHS trusts and GP fundholders.

The NAO carries out the audit of the summarised accounts of the NHS, as well as a number of health service agencies and NDPBs. Both the NAO and the Audit Commission carry out value for money studies within the NHS.

The Audit Commission prepares its own accounts on an accruals basis, complying where appropriate with the Companies Acts and accounting standards. These accounts are audited by the NAO and published.

❏ Scottish Accounts Commission

The Commission for Local Authority Accounts in Scotland carries out about half the Scottish local authority audits. The remainder are carried out by accountancy firms.

❏ Registered auditor

At present the only registered auditors are those recognised under Schedule 11 to the Companies Act 1989. These are mainly the professional firms of Chartered Accountants or Certified Accountants mentioned above, although there are also 500 registered auditors who are members of the Association of Authorised Public Accountants. All companies are required to use a registered auditor, though the 1994 Finance Bill is removing the need for small companies to be audited.

Large charities, with income over £100,000, may also be required under the Charities Act 1993, section 43, to have their accounts audited by a registered auditor, unless they are audited by the NAO or the Audit Commission.

❏ Independent examiner

The Charities Act allows small charities to be audited by an independent examiner. Such a person needs no professional qualification.

The audit report

The purpose of external audit is to provide an opinion on the reliability of the accounts presented by the organisation to users. This opinion will be expressed in the audit certificate or audit report. The exact form of the report depends on the type of organisation and the resulting auditing standards that are being followed by the auditors.

❏ National Audit Office

An example of an NAO audit report is shown in Figure 9.2.

Patent Office
Certificate and Report of the Comptroller and Auditor General.

I certify that I have examined the financial statements on pages 51 to 59 in accordance with the Government Trading Funds Act 1973 and the National Audit Office auditing standards.

In my opinion the financial statements on pages 51 to 59 give a true and fair view of the state of affairs of the Patent Office Trading Fund at 31 March 1993 and of Its surplus and cash flows for the year then ended and have been properly prepared in accordance with the Government Trading Funds Act 1973 and directions made thereunder by the Treasury.

I have no observations to make on these financial statements.

John Bourn Comptroller and Auditor General 8 July 1993
National Audit Office

Figure 9.2 Patent Office: NAO Audit Report.

There are four key points for a user of the accounts to check in this report:

- the page numbers covered

  information outside these pages has not been audited. Unaudited information for the Patent Office includes the annual report, the foreword to the accounts, the accounts directions and non-financial targets. The foreword is checked to ensure that it is consistent with the accounts

- the scope of the audit

  the relevant legislation and auditing standards which have been followed

- the opinion

  here the accounts give a true and fair view, and have been properly prepared. This is the judgement of the C&AG based on the work done, not a certificate

- no observations

  so this is a clean report.

NAO auditing standards are published, and cover two areas, operational and reporting. They lay down standards for the method of work, the approach, and how to report findings.

The operational standard covers:

- planning, controlling and reporting
- audit evidence
- accounting systems
- internal controls
- review of financial statements.

The reporting standard deals with both certification and value for money audits. The certification audit part covers:

- certification of financial statements
- qualification of certificate
- revenue accounts
- stock and store accounts.

❏ Accountancy firm audit

An audit report from an accountancy firm will follow the requirements of Statement of Auditing Standard 600. SAS 600 came into effect for accounts ending on or after 30 September 1993. The NAO will be adopting SAS 600.

Figure 9.3, shows an example of an audit report from an accountancy firm.

Although at first sight this might seem more complex, and perhaps suggest that there were problems, in fact it covers the same four points as the Patent Office style report, but adds:

- a reminder of the respective responsibilities of the board members and auditors
- an explanation of the nature of an audit.

This report is made a little more complicated by the fact that it needs to refer to the accounts of the Post Office and those of its separate businesses.

It refers to different auditing standards, those issued by the Auditing Practices Board (APB). The APB is composed of accounting practitioners from all the accountancy institutes, members of the NAO and Audit Commission, as well as non-practitioners from business, the law and academics. The Department of Trade and Industry provides a non-voting member. These auditing standards are being published in stages, and will cover:

- responsibility, including going concern
- planning, controlling and recording

- accounting systems and internal control
- evidence
- using the work of others
- reporting - including SAS600.

Report of the auditors

to the Secretary of State for Trade and Industry on the accounts of the Post Office and its constituent businesses

We have audited the accounts of the Post Office set out on pages 42 to 56 and each of the Post Office's constituent businesses set out on pages 57 to 85 which have been prepared on the basis of the accounting policies set out on pages 42 and 43.

Respective responsibilities of Board Members and auditors

As described on page 40 the Board Members are responsible for the preparation of the accounts. It is our responsibility to form an independent opinion, based on our audit, on those accounts and to report our opinion to you.

Basis of opinions

We conducted our audit in accordance with Auditing Standards issued by the Auditing Practices Board. An audit includes examination, on a test basis, of evidence relevant to the amounts and disclosures in the accounts. It also includes an assessment of the significant estimates and judgements made by the Board Members in the preparation of the accounts, and of whether the accounting policies are appropriate to the circumstances of the Post Office and its constituent businesses, consistently applied and adequately disclosed.

We planned and performed our audit so as to obtain all the information and explanations which we considered necessary in order to provide us with sufficient evidence to give reasonable assurance that the accounts are free from material misstatement, whether caused by fraud or other irregularity or error. In forming our opinions we also evaluated the overall adequacy of the presentation of information in the accounts.

Opinions

In our opinion the accounts set out on pages 42 to 56 give a true and fair view of the state of affairs of the Post Office Corporation and of the Group at 28 March 1993 and of the results of the Post Office Corporation and of the Group for the financial year then ended and have been properly prepared in accordance with Section 75(1) of the British Telecommunications Act 1981 together with the requirements made and directions and approvals given by the Secretary of State for Trade and Industry, under the Act and as reproduced on page 99.

In addition, in our opinion the accounts set out on pages 57 to 85 give a true and fair view of the state of affairs of each of the constituent businesses of the Post Office at 28 March 1993 and of their results for the financial year then ended and have been properly prepared in accordance with the requirements made and directions and approvals given by the Secretary of State for Trade and Industry, as reproduced on page 99.

Ernst + Young

—

Ernst & Young
CHARTERED ACCOUNTANTS
REGISTERED AUDITOR
LONDON

4 JUNE 1993

Figure 9.3 The Post Office Audit Report by an accountancy firm.

There are auditing guidelines for specific sectors, including Charities, Housing Associations, as well as one on the impact of regulations on public sector audits.

❏ Local authority audit

A local authority report will follow the format shown in Figure 9.4.

FINANCIAL STATEMENTS

OPINION OF THE AUDITORS

1. The audit of the Authority's accounts for the year ended 31 March 1993 has been carried out in accordance with Part III of the Local Government Finance Act 1982 and the Code of Audit Practice, and has been substantially completed.

2. The audit cannot be formally concluded, however, because:

    (a) The date for the exercise of public rights relating to these accounts has not yet been reached and any matters which may be raised by electors at the appropriate time have not necessarily been taken into account.

    (b) Audit procedures not directly relevant to this opinion, principally related to value for money studies, have not yet been completed.

3. In our opinion:

    (a) The statement of accounts set out on pages 4 to 24 presents fairly the financial position of the Authority at 31 March 1993 and its income and expenditure for the year then ended.

    (b) The summarised statement of accounts relating to the Superannuation Fund set out on pages 25 to 27 presents fairly the financial position of the Fund at 31 March 1993 and its income and expenditure for the year then ended.

Reut Mannich.

KPMG PEAT MARWICK
Registered Auditor
July 1993

Figure 9.4 Surrey County Council: audit report by an accountancy firm.

The scope of the audit here depends on the Code of Local Government Audit Practice. This code was last revised in 1990, and

> sets out the general duties of auditors, how they should conduct the audit and how they should report on results, in the form of the audit opinion, public interest reports and management letters.

The Code, as reported by the Audit Commission, 1993, requires auditors to give an independent assessment of:

- whether the statement of accounts presents fairly the financial position of the authority
- the general financial standing of the authority
- the adequacy of the financial systems
- the adequacy of arrangements in place for preventing and detecting fraud and corruption

- the performance of particular services
- the effectiveness of management arrangements.

In the Surrey statement, the second section of the report states that all the audit work is not yet complete. However, this does not prevent the opinion being reached.

Local authority accounts are not intended to show a true and fair view, rather to 'present fairly', and this is what the report concludes. This distinction may seem subtle, but it means that statements of standard accounting practice (SSAPs) and financial reporting standards (FRSs), which automatically apply to all 'true and fair' audits, do not automatically apply. Chapter 8 had more details on those standards and their implications.

Audit reports for other parts of the public sector will usually follow the format seen in the three examples above:

- scope
- restrictions (if any)
- opinion.

Organisations which produce two sets of accounts, historical and current cost, will have an opinion which comments on both sets of figures. An example is shown in Figure 9.5.

Report of the Auditors

To the Secretary of State for Trade and Industry

We have audited the accounts of British Coal Corporation on pages 42 to 73 in accordance with Auditing Standards.

In our opinion:

(a) the accounts give a true and fair view of the state of affairs of the Corporation at March 27 1993 and, in respect of the Corporation and their subsidiary undertakings regarded as a single entity, of the state of affairs at March 27 1993 and the results and statement of cash flows for the year then ended, and have been properly prepared in accordance with the direction of the Secretary of State for Trade and Industry on pages 75 and 76; and,

(b) the supplementary current cost information on page 74 has been properly prepared in accordance with the bases and methods described in note 2.

London	Ernst and Young
July 2 1993	Chartered Accountants
	Registered Auditor

Figure 9.5 Audit report covering both historical and current costs.

❏ Qualified audit reports

There are a number of factors which may result in an audit report's being qualified. Qualifications may arise because the scope of the auditors' examination has been limited, or because the auditors disagree with the treatment or disclosure of a matter in the accounts.

The accounts will be qualified if the auditors consider that the accounts may not or do not give a 'true and fair' or 'fair' view, or whatever view is formally specified as the requirement. Immaterial items will not affect the opinion, unless there are sufficient immaterial items to add up to a material problem.

Figure 9.6, may help to decipher the nature of the problem resulting in a qualified report:

| | Severity of problem | |
Reason for qualification	Material but not fundamental	Fundamental
Limitation of scope	'except for' possible adjustments	Unable to express an opinion
Disagreement	'except for'	Do not give a true and fair view

Figure 9.6 Reasons for qualified audit reports.

Looking at some qualified reports shows the different qualifications. The report on Ordnance Survey in Figure 9.7, draws two facts to the attention of the reader:

- 'except for the absence of any valuation of large scale maps' - this is a material but not fundamental disagreement. Ordnance Survey has not done something which it could have done, and which the NAO thinks it should have done, and the C&AG thinks that it has a material effect on the accounts

- there is no valuation of the database. Here the C&AG agrees with the presentation used, but feels that the readers of the accounts should be aware that such a valuable item is not included, and note 1.5 on page 21 might escape their attention.

The report for the Buying Agency, shown in Figure 9.8, states that there has been a limitation in the scope of the audit, in that the C&AG is uncertain that income was complete. This leads to a qualification, and the wording indicates that this is thought to be material but not fundamental. This certificate is followed by a two-page report explaining the circumstances behind the problem, what the Agency had done to minimise it and what the NAO did to quantify it.

Certificate Of The Comptroller And Auditor General

I certify that I have examined the financial statements on pages 18 to 28 in accordance with the Exchequer and Audit Departments Act 1921 and the National Audit Office auditing standards.

Except for the absence of any valuation of stocks of large scale maps described in my report, in my opinion the financial statements give a true and fair view of the state of affairs of Ordnance Survey at 31 March 1993 and of its deficit, total recognised losses and cash flows for the year then ended and have been properly prepared in accordance with Section 5 of the Exchequer and Audit Departments Act 1921 and directions made thereunder by the Treasury.

Without qualifying my opinion, I draw attention to Note 1.5 on page 21 of the accounts which sets out the reasons why no valuation is shown in the Balance Sheet for the National Topographic Database of geodetic networks and topographic information.

John Bourn
Comptroller and Auditor General

National Audit Office
7 July 1993.

Report Of The Comptroller And Auditor General

As in previous years, the Accounts for 1992/93 exclude any valuation of stocks of large scale maps. This practice represents a departure from the Statement of Standard Accounting Practice No. 9 which requires stock to be stated in the Balance Sheet at the lower of cost and net realisable value. Ordnance Survey have not quantified the effect of this departure on the grounds that the cost of doing so would outweigh the benefits. In my view the amounts likely to be involved are material to a true and fair view of the body's state of affairs and, as in previous years, I have qualified my certificate accordingly.

John Bourn
Comptroller and Auditor General

National Audit Office
7 July 1993.

Figure 9.7 Audit report: Ordnance Survey.

CERTIFICATE
OF THE COMPTROLLER AND
AUDITOR GENERAL

I certify that I have examined the financial statements on pages 13 to 21 in accordance with the Government Trading Funds Act 1973 and the National Audit Office auditing standards, except that, as explained in my report, set out on pages 23 and 24, I was unable to satisfy myself as to the completeness of call-off commission income.

Subject to any adjustments that I might have found to be necessary had I been able to satisfy myself as to the completeness of the amount of income due from call-off commission, in my opinion the financial statements give a true and fair view of the state of affairs of The Buying Agency at 31 December 1992 and of its surplus and cash flows for the year then ended and have been properly prepared in accordance with the Government Trading Funds Act 1973 and the Order made thereunder by the Secretary of State for the Environment.

John Bourn
Comptroller and Auditor General

National Audit Office
21 April 1993

Figure 9.8 Audit report: The Buying Agency.

The type of qualification thus needs to be studied to see whether it is material or fundamental. Most organisations will try to avoid a qualification, by changing their procedures or providing extra information for the auditors, so the qualifications which remain are only those that the organisation cannot or will not do something about.

The report on the Development Board for Rural Wales accounts 1992-93 shown in Figure 9.9 appears satisfactory.

BWRDD DATBLYGU CYMRU WLEDIG

DEVELOPMENT BOARD FOR RURAL WALES ACCOUNTS 1992–93

Certificate of the Comptroller and Auditor General

I certify that I have examined the financial statements on pages 6 to 24 in accordance with Section 14 of the Development of Rural Wales Act 1976 and the National Audit Office auditing standards.

In my opinion the financial statements give a true and fair view of the state of affairs of the Development Board for Rural Wales at 31 March 1993 and of its deficit and cash flows for the year then ended and have been properly prepared in accordance with Section 14 of the Development of Rural Wales Act 1976 and determination's made thereunder by the Secretary of State for Wales with the approval of Treasury.

John Bourn
Comptroller and Auditor General

See also Report of the Comptroller and Auditor General

Figure 9.9 The report on the Development Board for Rural Wales.

However, this report omits the final paragraph seen in the Patent Office report, the 'no observations' statement, and does refer to the report of the C&AG. This second report runs to over 4 pages, and covers problems with housing activities, car leasing and other staff benefits. These problems have <u>not</u> affected the true and fair view, but have resulted in unacceptable practice and irregular payments.

Finally, just as accounts can be published in Welsh so can Audit Reports (Figure 9.10)

❏ Error and fraud

The primary purpose of the external audit work is to collect evidence to form an opinion. The auditor must decide how much work needs to be carried out. The final risk of the accounts containing material error consists of three separate components of risk:

> **TYSTYSGRIF AC ADRODDIAD Y RHEOLWR A'R ARCHWILYDD CYFFREDINOL**
>
> Tystiaf fy mod wedi archwilio'r datganiadau ariannol ar dudalennau 33 i 44 yn unol â Deddf Adrannau'r Trysorlys ac Archwilio Cyfrifon 1921 a safonau archwilio'r Swyddfa Archwilio Genedlaethol.
>
> Yn fy marn i dengys y datganiadau ariannol hyn ddarlun gwir a theg o sefyllfa Cadw ar 31 Mawrth 1993 ac o'r gwariant net a'r llifoedd arian am y flwyddyn a orffennodd bryd hynny ac y maent wedi eu paratoi'n briodol yn unol â Deddf Adrannau'r Trysorlys ac Archwilio Cyfrifon 1921 a'r hyn a bennwyd o dan y ddeddf honno gan y Trysorlys.
>
> Nid oes gennyf unrhyw sylwadau i'w gwneud ar y datganiadau ariannol hyn.
>
>
> John Bourn
> Rheolydd ac Archwilydd Cyffredinol
> Swyddfa Archwilio Genedlaethol
> 16 Tachwedd 1993

Figure 9.10 The Welsh version of the report on Cadw (Welsh Historic Monuments).

- inherent risk - the likelihood of an error being made in the first place
- control risk - the risk that the internal controls and internal audit will fail to prevent or correct the error
- audit risk - the chance that the audit, because it does not test every transaction and every balance, will fail to find the error.

The auditors' assessment of the level of inherent and control risk will then affect the type and amount of audit work done to minimise the audit risk.

Individual errors may not be material, but if they reveal that, say 1 in 20 sales invoices are incorrect, then the error rate will be projected from the sample tested onto the whole population to see if there is likely to be a material error overall.

Auditors cannot be 100% confident that they have reached the right opinion, for two reasons. Firstly, the accounts are prepared to be true and fair, with estimates and assumptions, and not to be correct. Secondly, it would be physically impossible for the auditors to check every transaction and balance, and their work must be based on samples. As it is impossible for the auditors to have 100% confidence that material error has not escaped them, 95% confidence is generally accepted as a reasonable compromise between too much work and too much risk. This means that there is a small chance that the final accounts contain undetected material error. It also means that it is possible that many immaterial errors may still be there.

The responsibility for prevention and detection of fraud lies with the management of the organisation, not with the auditors. If a fraud has resulted in a material error, audit procedures should have been designed to have a reasonable expectation of detecting material misstatement and consequently any fraud that may have been the cause.

Most auditors will write a management letter, to the management of the organisation, pointing out any problems they have encountered and any possible changes to the accounting systems to improve control. The letter is not made public, but it should increase the value of the external audit.

❏ Value for money audit

As mentioned earlier, both the National Audit Office and the Audit Commission have a statutory right to investigate the economy, efficiency and effectiveness with which public bodies spend public money.

The NAO conduct enquiries into government departments, agencies and other public bodies. Large spending departments such as the Ministry of Defence may have several enquiries in a year, while much smaller organisations may go for decades without being studied individually. Examples of recent reports on other parts of the public sector are:

- Grant Maintained Schools in England : Financial Controls (1993, HC577)
- University Purchasing in England (1993, HC635)
- Housing Corporation : Financial Management of Housing Associations (1993, HC892)
- Repeat Prescribing by General Medical Practitioners in England (1993, HC897.)

Most NAO value for money reports concern an individual organisation, or the relationship between organisations. Occasionally, reports cover one topic over a number of departments. A recent example is *Management of Telephone Services* (1993, HC931). The NAO may not question the value for money of policies, only their implementation.

By contrast, the Audit Commission's national reports cover topics which relate to a number of local authorities or health authorities. Recent topics include :

- Developing Local Authority Housing Strategy
- Children First : A Study of Hospital Services.

These reports enable the performance of one organisation to be compared to others. At the local level, reports will be issued to individual organisations by the NAO and the Audit Commission.

References

Audit Commission
Report and accounts 1993
HMSO, London   1993

Audit Commission
Code of Local Government Audit Practice
HMSO, London   1990

Auditing Practices Board (APB)
Statement of Auditing Standards 100 (exposure draft) - Objectives and general principles governing an audit of financial statements
APB, London   1993

Auditing Practices Board (APB)
Statement of Auditing Standards 500 (exposure draft) - Considering the work of internal audit
APB, London   1993

Auditing Practices Board (APB)
Statement of Auditing Standards 600 - Auditors' reports on financial statements
APB, London   1993

H M Treasury
Government Internal Audit Manual
HMSO, London   1988

Institute of Chartered Accountants in England and Wales
Accountancy
ICAEW, London   July, 1994

Lopez LJ
In re Kingston Cotton Mill Company
Court of Appeal [1896 2Ch. 279]

National Audit Office
Auditing Standards
NAO   undated

National Audit Office
Grant Maintained Schools in England: Financial Control
HMSO, London   1993

National Audit Office
University Purchasing in England
HMSO, London   1993

National Audit Office
Housing Corporation: Financial Management of Housing Associations
HMSO, London   1993

National Audit Office
Repeat Prescribing by General Medical Practitioners in England
HMSO, London   1993

National Audit Office
Management of Telephone Services
HMSO, London   1993

Chapter 10

Measuring financial performance

There can be no economy where there is no efficiency. *(Disraeli, 1868)*

Once an organisation has prepared a full set of accounts, which meet all the disclosure requirements and have been audited, the accounts will provide a picture of the organisation's financial state of affairs and of how it has performed over the period. However, this will be a static picture, and in order to begin to understand what has happened, comparison needs to be made with:

- a series of pictures over time
- any targets set
- the pictures of other similar organisations.

All sets of accounts will provide comparative information for the previous year, unless the organisation is in its first year. The comparative figures appear on the operating account, balance sheet and cash flow statement as well as in the notes. Information on the financial targets that an organisation has been set will also appear in its accounts. However, comparisons with other organisations will not be shown in the accounts, though they could be included in an annual report.

The importance of financial targets was stated by HM Treasury (1993):

> Financial targets, which are usually set for three year periods, are the primary control on the (nationalised) industries.

Overall financial performance

In the public sector the key financial targets, covering overall financial performance, are likely to be in the following four categories:

- breakeven
- cost recovery
- return on sales
- return on assets.

❑ Breakeven

Breakeven is achieved when income and costs exactly equal each other, and there is neither surplus nor deficit. This is also described as full cost recovery. Many fees and charges operations are tasked with achieving breakeven. *The Fees and Charges Guide* (HM Treasury 1992) states:

> The financial objective should normally be full cost recovery.

All Trading Funds are required by legislation to break even as a minimum. Section 4 (1) Government Trading Funds Act 1973, as amended, states:

> it shall be his duty to manage the funded operations so that the revenue of the fund ...is not less than sufficient, taking one year with another, to meet outgoings which are properly chargeable to revenue account.

Similarly, Section 10(1) National Health Service and Community Care Act 1990 contains the following:

> Every NHS Trust shall ensure that its revenue is not less than sufficient, taking one financial year with another, to meet outgoings properly chargeable to revenue account.

The Central Office of Information is the only trading fund which currently has breakeven as its main financial target. It has actually achieved a small surplus each year, amounting to a return on sales of 0.02% in 1992-93. Among the nationalised industries, only the Parcelforce division of the Post Office has a breakeven target. British Coal is targeted to move towards profitability.

❑ Cost recovery

If an organisation cannot achieve full cost recovery, i.e. breakeven, then it may be set targets for cost recovery of less than 100%, but equally the target may be to achieve more than 100% where that is feasible.

Fees and charges operations are permitted to charge less than full cost when there is:

- excess capacity which cannot be easily disposed of
- fluctuating demand, so less may be charged in 'off-peak' periods.

Prices higher than full cost may be charged when there is:

- excess demand (until extra capacity is obtained)
- fluctuating demand, when there are peak periods

Agencies operating on-vote, are most likely to be achieving less than full cost recovery, otherwise they would not require vote finance to balance their cash flow.

Cost recovery can be calculated simply as:

$$\frac{\text{Turnover}}{\text{Costs}}$$

Ordnance Survey is set four cost recovery targets as shown in Figure 10.1.

Category of business	Objective	Achievement 1992/93
Core	65% by 1992/93	59%
Small scales and special products	maximise revenue:	
	not less than 110%	91%
Public sector repayment	at least 100%	108%
Overall cost recovery	70%	65%

Figure 10.1 Ordnance Survey cost recovery targets .

This statement from the accounts provides more information than can be obtained by calculation from the figures shown in the accounts, as the turnover and costs are not identified separately by category there. It clearly shows which category is intended to be subsidised, which is only the core (detailed mapping.) In fact, the results show that the small scale products have not been as successful as was planned.

Caledonian MacBrayne, a nationalised industry, has a cost recovery target, namely to recover at least 59% of its operating costs from fares income in 1993/94.

❏ Return on sales

Return on sales involves a simple comparison between the surplus and turnover, both of which are disclosed in the operating account. For example, using hypothetical figures:

	Year 1	Year 2	Year 3
Turnover	1,000	1,600	2,000
Surplus	50	80	100

The return on sales for each year, calculated as:

$$\frac{\text{Surplus}}{\text{Turnover}}$$

| is: | 5% | 5% | 5% |

This is also sometimes referred to as the profit margin. In the public sector this form of target would normally be used only where a profit is feasible but where, for some reason, a target in the form of a return on assets, described below, does not make sense.

An example might be organisations whose main purpose in life is to reduce costs to their customers. Any increases in surpluses would be achieved only as a result of higher costs to their customers.

The Buying Agency has a target to achieve a surplus which is 1½% of the total value of goods and services procured through it. In recent years results have been:

     1992 - 2.5%   1991 - 2.3%

As a recognition of the fact that the 1992 surplus was higher than the target, The Buying Agency surrendered all of the surplus to the Consolidated Fund.

❏ Return on assets

Return on assets concentrates on the relationship between the level of surplus and the value of the net assets of the organisation. It thus links information from the operating account and the balance sheet. In the hypothetical example above, this organisation seemed to be performing consistently, with a return on sales of 5% each year. However, if the value of the assets is considered, the view of its performance may change. For example, assume that the values of net assets were as follows:

Net assets	500	1,000	2,000

The return on assets, calculated as:

$$\frac{\text{Surplus}}{\text{Net assets}}$$

is:	10%	8%	5%

This indicates a decreasing return on the resources tied up in the organisation, as more resources have gone into the organisation each year without a commensurate increase in the surplus.

The return on assets, or return on capital, tends to be referred to as the primary ratio, because it is often the first ratio calculated in examining the performance of companies. It is more fully calculated as:

$$\frac{\text{Surplus before interest}}{\text{Net assets}} \quad \text{or} \quad \frac{\text{Surplus after interest}}{\text{Net assets plus loans}}$$

This calculation is further refined by not using the net assets in the balance sheet at the end of the year, but using the average of the assets at the beginning and end. In the hypothetical example used above the calculation for years 2 and 3 would be:

$$\text{Year 2} \quad \frac{\text{Surplus}}{\text{Average net assets}} = \frac{80}{(500+1,000)/2} = \frac{80}{750} = \mathbf{10.67\%}$$

$$\text{Year 3} \quad \frac{\text{Surplus}}{\text{Average net assets}} = \frac{100}{(1,000+2,000)/2} = \frac{100}{1,500} = \mathbf{6.67\%}$$

These give higher results, as they reflect the fact that the surplus was earned over the year as a whole, during which the balance sheet values were growing.

Return on assets is a very common way of setting a target for public sector organisations. The following are examples of targets set for 1993/94.

Trading Funds:

Statutory monopolies:	Vehicle Inspectorate	
	Companies House	all 6%
	Patent Office	
Others	Fire Service College	6%
Commercial operation	Royal Mint	12½%

NHS trusts

6%

Nationalised industries:

Civil Aviation Authority	8%
Nuclear Electric	13 - 15%
Post Office - Royal Mail Letters	16%
Post Office Counters	9.3%

The targets for the Royal Mint, the Civil Aviation Authority and Royal Mail Letters were all set as an average annual return over three years.

Some of these targets are set in terms of historical cost, some in current cost, some modified historical cost. If comparison is made with an equivalent private sector organisation, then care should be taken to ensure that the bases are comparable.

The actual returns achieved vary from target. In 1993, Vehicle Inspectorate achieved 12.8%, Companies House a deficit, the Patent Office 7%, the Royal Mint 22.4% and the Civil Aviation Authority 15.1%. NHS trusts also showed a spread, with 18 out of 119 in deficit, while 81 achieved or exceeded their 6% target. (CIPFA 1994)

Local authority direct labour and direct service organisations (DLOs and DSOs) were previously required to make 6% return. They are now required to break even.

Other aspects of financial performance

The types of target considered so far are basically options for single measures of aggregate performance of an organisation. Normally, only one of them would be used for a single organisation. However, there are other financial measures which can be derived from the accounts and which supplement the overall measure, concentrating on particular aspects of financial performance. The following sections look at the three such aspects considered to be most important for the public sector:

- unit costs
- financing and borrowing
- balance sheet management.

❏ Unit costs

The unit cost, which is an indicator of both efficiency (how well inputs are converted into outputs) and economy (the choice and purchase of inputs) is simply calculated as:

$$\frac{\text{Relevant costs}}{\text{Units achieved}}$$

This is not purely a financial measure, as it depends on the non-financial information on units. It is a good measure of efficiency, as it compares the input cost with the output achieved. Examples of unit cost targets are:

Companies House	- real unit cost reduction 2% per annum
UK Passport Agency	- real unit cost reduction
Driving Standards Agency	- unit cost of £22.48 for car test
London Underground	- reduce operating costs per train mile to £16.20 by 1995/96.

Vehicle Inspectorate has a more complicated measure. It is set an aggregated cost efficiency index (ACE), which for 1992-93 was 1.7%. The accounts explain it as:

> Very broadly, the ACE mechanism compares the cost of total output in a given year, with the amount the same output would have cost in the previous year, using the previous year's unit cost outturn adjusted for inflation. It does this for each of the major schemes. These indicators are then aggregated to form a single index.

Unit costs calculated on an accruals basis provide a more accurate reflection of all the costs incurred than cash costs would. Because the unit cost involves the non-financial information on units, it is usually outside the scope of the statutory accounts and not audited. The audit may be extended if the unit cost figures are needed to calculate bonus payments.

❑ Financing and borrowing

When it comes to controlling the burden which public sector bodies place on the economy, a method used for some organisations is to set them an External Finance Limit (EFL). This method is used for trading funds, NHS trusts and nationalised industries.

External finance is a cash control, not a control based on accruals accounts. It is the difference between two large cash flows; namely the cash an organisation spends (including capital expenditure) and the cash generated from its operations. A relatively small variation in either of these may result in a proportionately larger change in external finance. This External Financing Requirement (EFR) is met by either borrowing or grant, or some combination of the two.

The EFR may be positive or negative. If negative it indicates that the organisation is repaying debt to the Treasury or its parent department, or accumulating financial assets.

A target for the EFL will be set in the Public Expenditure Survey, covering three years ahead. Nationalised industries are expected to show outturn against target EFL in their annual reports, not in their accounts.

❑ Balance sheet management

Financial performance indicators can be used to see how an organisation is managing its balance sheet. The return on assets will show how this has been achieved overall. Individual measures can then be calculated to see how the components of the balance sheet have been managed. The commonly used measures are:

- fixed asset turnover
- debtor days
- creditor days
- stock days
- debtors and work in progress investment.

Fixed asset turnover

This gives an indication of how busy the organisation is for the level of fixed assets tied up. An organisation which uses a lot of fixed assets, such as a manufacturing agency, will have a low value, for example Ordnance Survey has a figure of 1.43. An organisation with few fixed assets relative to turnover is the Central Office of Information which had a figure of 83.7 in 1993.

This measure can be used to set a target relating to investment in new fixed assets, so that justification for their purchase could depend on a prediction of a certain increase in turnover. (It should be emphasised that this would certainly not be the only justification for investment.)

Debtor days

Debtor days is defined as

$$\frac{\text{Trade debtors} \times 365 \text{ days}}{\text{Turnover}} \quad \text{which is equal to} \quad \frac{\text{Uncollected debts}}{\text{Daily turnover}}$$

This shows how long, on average, the debtors have been outstanding. It will seem lower than the reality if there is a significant proportion of cash sales. The figure of trade debtors represents the position at one particular point in time, at the year end. It can be distorted by the fact that, at the end of March, many public sector organisations may be making or holding back payment depending on their own cash flow situation.

Debtor days calculated from accounts for 1993 show a wide range. Examples are:

ITC	6 days
S4C	12 days
Civil Aviation Authority	43 days
Forestry Commission	47 days
HMSO	54 days
Ordnance Survey	62 days

The figure can be compared to the organisation's normal terms of trade to see if all debts are being collected as quickly as they should be. Most organisations will suffer an interest penalty (real or notional) on uncollected debts. For example, a £1,200 debtor who should pay after 30 days but in fact pays after 60 days will cost £10 extra in interest, if interest rates are 10%. The organisation will have to decide whether it can build the extra £10 into its prices, or whether it should make the effort to collect the debt after 30 days.

Many public sector organisations insist on payment from the public in advance and would not have any trade debtors or debtor days.

Creditor days

Creditor days are calculated as :

$$\frac{\text{Trade creditors} \times 365 \text{ days}}{\text{Cost of sales}} \quad \text{which is equal to} \quad \frac{\text{Unpaid suppliers}}{\text{Daily cost of sales}}$$

As few accounts publish a cost of sales figure, it may be easier to use total operating costs, excluding staff costs. The actual figures calculated from the accounts again show a wide range in 1993:

Forestry Commission	6 days
ITC	13 days
Ordnance Survey	21 days
HMSO	54 days

Companies House disclose in their 1993 accounts that :

Payment of Bills

The average time taken to pay suppliers was 33 days, including suppliers of overheads and capital; the calculation excludes recoverable VAT.

This figure may be different from creditor days as defined above because the figure for trade creditors used in the ratio of creditor days applies only to one particular point in time, namely the year end. The average time taken to pay suppliers may be calculated by looking at how long on average it took to pay individual invoices.

Stock days

Stock days are calculated as:

$$\frac{\text{Stock}}{\text{Cost of sales}} \times 365 \text{ days}$$

This ratio shows on average how long stock has been waiting in the production process. There are few public sector organisations with significant holdings of stocks. Their 1993 accounts enable the following figures to be calculated:

HMSO	31	days
British Rail	51	days
British Coal	61	days
Ordnance Survey	102	days
Royal Mint	420	days

Again, it may be necessary to combine a number of costs if no cost of sales figure is published.

Debtors and work in progress investment (net investment)

Debtors and WIP investment is calculated as:

$$\frac{\text{Debtors and work in progress} \times 365 \text{ days}}{\text{Turnover}}$$

This shows how much is tied up, for a service organisation, in work which is either billed to customers and not yet paid, or work which has been started but not yet completed and billed. A figure of 80 days for this indicator can be calculated from the accounts of the Central Office of Information.

Non-financial targets

Organisations are almost certain to be set targets for their performance in terms other than financial ones. These may be for:

- quality of service, including accuracy, waiting times
- effectiveness
- efficiency
- volume of output.

The National Audit Office (1989) said

> The setting of genuine indicators of Agency performance... is a mandatory requirement for establishing an Agency.

Successful management of the organisation will depend on the achievement of these non-financial targets as well as the chosen financial measures. As they are based on non-financial data they do not form part of the accounts, but will be in the annual report. Some Citizens Charter performance indicators, set out by the Audit Commission, and Patients Charter indicators in the NHS are, however, required to be audited.

References

CIPFA
NHS Trust Database, as reported in "Public Finance"   1994

Disraeli
Letter to constituents
in *Letters*   3 October 1868

H M Treasury
The Fees and Charges Guide
HMSO, London   1992

H M Treasury
Executive Agencies: a guide to setting targets and measuring performance
HMSO, London   1992

H M Treasury
Public Expenditure : Statistical Supplement to the Financial Statement and Budget Report 1994/95
HMSO, London   1993

National Audit Office
The Next Steps Initiative (HC410)
HMSO, London   1989

Chapter 11

Creative accounting

Round numbers are always false. *(Samuel Johnson, 1778)*

The purpose of this chapter is not to provide those preparing accounts with many ways in which to mislead the readers. Competent finance directors will be aware of what is covered here, and probably of much more. The reason for including this subject is so that users of the accounts, who may not be as financially literate as those preparing them, can at least be on the look out and ask appropriate questions.

Cash accounting is precise, in that the amount of cash spent, received and left at the end of a period can be checked. Accruals accounting depends on many judgements, and the conclusion of the auditors can be no more than that the accounts are true and fair, or fairly present the information.

There are many reasons why organisations may wish to have an interest in pushing the figures in the accounts in a particular direction. Here are a few which may be relevant to the public sector:

- by reducing the value of the net assets on the balance sheet, the managers of the organisation will reduce the interest (real or notional) that they have to pay on the corresponding debt

- by reducing the value of net assets prior to privatisation, the managers make it easier for them to succeed in a management buy-out, or make it easier to show improvement post-privatisation

- by influencing the results management may affect their own performance-related pay

- by depressing the results the organisation may increase the funding it can obtain from central government, or from charitable sources

- by improving the results the organisation may be able to justify its continued existence

- a smooth trend in results may look more satisfactory than an erratic pattern

- an organisation subject to corporation tax may wish to reduce surpluses to minimise its tax liability.

These reasons may push in different directions, so there will be no way of telling automatically for an individual organisation which way it might wish to massage the figures. It is best simply to think hard when looking at any set of accounts that the figures could be moved either way.

The examples in this chapter of actual practice from accounts have been chosen as illustrations of what might be possible. They **Do Not** imply that those accounts have actually been subject to creative accounting or manipulation. They illustrate the scope for presenting different results within the range of practices which have been considered acceptable, and show the need to look carefully at how accounts have been prepared. It can be dangerous to take the financial results at face value.

Creative accounting and creative financing

It is important to be clear that not every 'dodgy' financial practice in which an organisation might indulge actually falls under the heading of creative accounting. On the whole, creative accounting is the term used to describe accounting adjustments made to events which have already taken place. According to Naser (1993):

> Creative accounting is the transformation of financial accounting figures from what they actually are to what preparers desire by taking advantage of the existing rules and/or ignoring some or all of them.

Creative *financing* is where the actual events are conducted in such a way as to have a particular impact on the accounts, either on the surplus or on the balance sheet. Examples are:

- sale and leaseback of fixed assets, where the result is that a fixed asset becomes cash. This gives rise to income in that year. However, to carry on using the asset there will be a rental cost rather than depreciation in later years. A significant improvement in income in one year may be at the expense of slightly higher costs in each future year. This has been used with parking meters, as well as with more typical fixed assets
- payment of creditors on the last day of the accounting period. Large amounts move out of cash to pay off the creditors, particularly on 31 March. The effect on net current assets is nil, but the reduction in creditors and cash is significant. The cash effect may be particularly important if the organisation is controlled by its cash spend or borrowings
- prepayment of expenses, such as air tickets, acts in the same way as early payment of creditors

- delaying payment to suppliers will maximise cash, minimise a bank overdraft and may enable the organisation to stay within a spending limit

- 'bed and breakfast' treatment of fixed asset investments. These cannot be shown at market value where this is more than cost. By selling the investment and immediately buying it back, on the last day of the year, the gain is realised and the investment can be included at the higher amount

- borrowing cash in order to invest it at a higher interest rate, ('arbitrage.') Western Isles obtained 5/16 % interest difference on the money it borrowed and invested in BCCI. This will improve the result shown by the operating account, net current assets will be unaffected but the risk is much higher than before the transaction

- factoring debts, whereby debtors are 'sold' to another organisation and a proportion of the debt is received immediately as cash. Debtor days improve and cash looks healthier, but the organisation may still run the risk of bad debts

- obtaining stock on consignment, where the ownership of the stock remains with the supplier, or parent department, until the point at which it is used. This will reduce stock and creditors

- obtaining the use of fixed assets by short-term leases, which do not need to be capitalised.

Massaging the operating account

	Increase in income or cost	**Decrease in income or cost**
Turnover	Change point of sale	Change point of sale
Cost of sales	Reduce closing stock and WIP valuation	Increase closing stock and WIP valuation
Pension costs	Increase provision	Use actuarial valuation to allow a 'holiday'
Repairs	Make provision for future costs	Treat as fixed assets
Depreciation	Reduce expected life Reduce expected residual value	Increase life
	Reduce capitalisation threshold	Increase threshold
Taxation	Provide more deferred tax on timing differences	Provide less deferred tax

Figure 11.1 Accounting decisions to change the surplus.

There are various ways in which particular accounting decisions can increase or reduce the surplus. Some of the most common are summarised in Figure 11.1. The less obvious elements from Figure 11.1 are now explained in more detail.

Point of sale

The point of sale is the point at which a sale is deemed to take place. This may be obvious when the cash and goods or service change hands at the same time, but is less obvious if there a time lag. Such delay will occur in organisations carrying out a long-term research programme, designing and supplying I T equipment, receiving a statutory fee in advance of providing a service or simply providing a service which spans the period end. The choice of point of sale is a crucial decision, since once a sale is included, the surplus on it can also be included. The accounting policies in accounts rarely disclose exactly how the point of sale has been arrived at, so a change could be made without it being evident.

Pension costs

A higher provision for pension costs may be made by re-assessing the liability to pay pensions. The Ordnance Survey accounts examined in chapters 5 and 6 include an exceptional charge of £11m for the pensions of staff who retired early. If the staff had continued to work their salaries would have been spread over future years.

The pension fund revaluation and holiday can be achieved if the organisation has its own pension fund. It can then use a surplus on an actuarial valuation in a number of ways. One is to reduce the organisation's own contributions while continuing the staff contributions at their previous level. Clearly it is right to undertake actuarial valuations from time to time and to reflect the conclusions in the accounts. However, there is a degree of choice in when to undertake such revaluations and how to deal with any resultant surplus.

The capital and revenue expenditure threshold

The threshold between capital and revenue expenditure, between fixed assets and repairs, is a crucial one. If the threshold is reduced from £5,000 per item to £1,000, there will be more fixed assets, more depreciation and less cost of re-pairs. If the threshold is increased from £5,000 to £10,000 then there will be fewer fixed assets and lower depreciation, but a higher cost of repairs. The actual thresh-old used by an organisation is very rarely declared in the accounting policies, so such a change would be difficult to detect

The choice as to whether certain costs should be treated as fixed assets can be significant. British Rail in 1992-93 capitalised infrastructure which had previously been written off as it was incurred, the net effect being to increase the opening value of fixed assets from £250m to £1,607m. The infrastructure costs had already been written off in full in earlier years and now, as a result of the change, there was an increase in the depreciation charge for 1992-93 and later years.

There will also be a reduction in track maintenance costs in 1992-93 and the future, but the overall effect of the changes is unlikely to be neutral as far as the operating account is concerned. The motivation behind this change at British Rail is almost certainly related to the progress towards privatisation, and the setting up of Railtrack, as a separate division to manage the infrastructure. The accounts arguably now give a fairer picture of all the assets.

Deferred tax

The options on deferred tax only relate to those organisations which are liable to Corporation tax. SSAP 15, as described in Chapter 8, states that deferred tax should be accounted for to the extent that it is probable that it will be payable or receivable. This leaves the actual determination of how much deferred tax to provide to the organisation. London Transport states in its accounting policy that:

> Provision is made for deferred taxation arising from timing differences between profits as computed for taxation purpose and profits as stated in the accounts, to the extent that the liability will be payable in the foreseeable future.

This is standard wording, and complies with SSAP 15. However, the note to the accounts states:

> No provision for timing differences has been made.

What is more, no contingent liability has been disclosed. Does London Transport have any liability, contingent or actual, to deferred tax? The detail of the note indicates that it has, but it is not quantified in the accounts.

Choice of cost method

The choice of cost method - historical, modified historical or current cost - will have a fundamental impact on the results. British Telecom adopted current cost while a nationalised industry, but after privatisation changed to historical cost. The effect was higher profits and lower assets, thus boosting the results in the eyes of the shareholders and improving the return on assets.

The balance sheet

Many of the ways of affecting the operating account above have a knock-on effect to the balance sheet. Some other common choices which can affect the balance sheet are summarised in Figure 11.2.

	Increase in item	**Decrease in item**
Fixed assets	Capitalise interest Reduce depreciation Reduce threshold Value property	Increase depreciation Value property
Intangibles	Include	Exclude
Stock	Reduce provisions Increase overheads in work in progress	Increase provisions
Debtors	Reduce provision for doubtful debts	Increase provision for doubtful debts
Taxation	Full provision for deferred tax	Reduced provision for deferred tax
Accruals	Accrue contingencies	

Figure 11.2 Accounting decisions to change the balance sheet.

Some of these are now described in more detail.

Capitalisation of interest

Interest may be capitalised where it forms part of the cost of acquiring a fixed asset, not if it forms part of the financing of the use of that fixed asset. Typically interest incurred while a building is being constructed could be capitalised, whereas the cost of the interest on the loan to buy the complete building could not. Capitalisation will reduce the interest charge in the operating account while the building is being completed, but will result in a higher depreciation charge over the life of the building. Unless...

Property valuation

Valuation of property can have a significant effect. The completed building on which the interest had been capitalised might then be revalued downwards. The fall in value would not appear in the operating account unless it was a 'permanent diminution in value', only in the statement of recognised gains and losses and in the notes to the accounts. An extreme example of this problem is Queens Moat Houses plc, which valued its hotels at 31 December 1991 at £2,079m, but by 31 December 1992 they had fallen to £738m. This significantly reduced the net asset value and improved the return on assets.

Public sector organisations may not all be as large as Queens Moat Houses, but the change in valuations can be just as significant. In April 1991, the Patent Office relocated to Wales, to a building which cost it £25.4m. When the Patent Office became a trading fund in October 1991, it had to finance the building, and it was then valued at a net current replacement cost of £17m.

Similarly, the Royal Mint relocated to Wales in 1974. When it became a trading fund on 1 April 1975, the valuation of the land and buildings was carried out:

> on the basis of capitalised current rental value for the factory and office accommodation of the same area and of broadly similar user requirements.

This resulted in a valuation of £2.3m, compared to a depreciated historical cost of £5.5m and replacement cost of £7.8m.

The Defence Research Agency accounts at 31 March 1992 show its total fixed assets as £615.8m. By 31 March 1993, the day before its vesting day as a trading fund, the value had fallen to £143.7m. Most of the fall was due to downward revaluations, and £445m was charged in the operating account, completely wiping out the operating surplus of £39m. This left DRA with a deficit for its first year of accruals accounting. It also had a clean starting point for trading fund status, and a tidy balance sheet.

Depreciation

Fixed assets may be depreciated to nil while still being in use. This may happen because too short an estimated life was chosen, or because the rate at which the asset was expected to be used has in fact slowed. To reflect what has happened, the asset should strictly be revalued, re-lifed and continue to be depreciated, but frequently such assets exist but are shown at nil value.

Fixed assets may exist, and not appear on the balance sheet for other reasons. Some executive agencies, such as Ordnance Survey, show the value of the property they occupy as a fixed asset on the balance sheet, while others, such as the National Physical Laboratory (NPL), only show the rent as a cost in the operating account. Similarly, NPL does not capitalise any cash spent improving the property, but writes it off in the year in which the cash is spent. This treatment is recommended by the Treasury guidance set out in *Accounting for capital assets* (1992), though it is closer to following legal form rather than commercial substance.

Leases may be operating leases (charged as rentals to the operating account or finance leases (capitalised as a fixed asset, with depreciation and interest charges).

A lease is classified as a finance lease in SSAP21 when the

> lease transfers substantially all the risks and rewards of ownership of an asset to the lessee.

A property lease with rent review to market levels every 5 years, (the situation of many Property Holdings leases on departmental estate and common user estate,) would probably not fall within this description. However, the dividing line between operating and finance leases is far from clear.

Stricter application of the definition of an asset as 'the right to future economic benefit' could potentially include <u>all</u> leased assets as fixed assets.

Intangibles

Intangibles, which may or may not be included in a balance sheet, have been discussed in Chapter 6.

In 1993, Companies House made full provision against the costs of developing computer based registers. This certainly lines up with prudence, but it also significantly increased their operating deficit from £202,000 to £2,341,000. One very bad year can then be followed by several good ones where the intangible item no longer needs to be amortised. For Companies House, if these costs had been amortised they would have been about £200,000 each year.

Other organisations may wish to exclude intangibles for other reasons. Trading funds would have to make a return, such as 6%, based on the value of all the fund's assets. Excluding intangibles before vesting day thus reduces the level of return required.

Work in progress

Where work in progress is significant, it has to be valued to include all the costs of getting it to its current state. These costs will, for service organisations, be primarily staff costs and overheads. The proportion of overheads included in WIP will affect its valuation, and one way of changing the overheads is to change the method of sharing out costs. Such a level of detail would not be disclosed in the accounting policies.

Debt provision

Provisions for bad and doubtful debts are one way of combining the optimism of accruals accounting, which includes income as soon as the services or goods have been provided, with prudence, which recognises that not every debtor will pay up. If one were very prudent and set up a high provision one year, releasing the provision would gradually boost the surpluses of subsequent years.

Contingencies

Contingencies, which are remote liabilities, may be included in the balance sheet as liabilities, even though the likelihood of payment is very remote. There is considerable scope for judgement as to what is an appropriate degree of prudence. Changes in that judgement can lead to sudden changes in financial results. An example might be the sudden inclusion by Ordnance Survey of the £24m provision for early retirement, which appeared suddenly in its 1992-93 accounts, even though £2m related to decisions made in previous years.

One contingency which has neither been provided for nor even quantified is London Transport's deferred tax mentioned above.

The Atomic Energy Authority accounts similarly include the note:

> There are contingent liabilities in respect of guarantees or contingencies arising in the normal course of business; and indemnities issued with the consent of the President of the Board of Trade and the Treasury in respect of claims for nuclear damage arising from nuclear matter in the course of carriage. (No material claims under these contingent liabilities are anticipated and accordingly no provision has been made.)

Other commitments and contingencies which may escape disclosure are:

* capital commitments
* costs of abandonment or restoration
* legal liabilities.

And for something really creative

> Commercial accounting systems were in place for the year to 31 March 1993, and, although the Agency remained Vote-funded, trading was simulated throughout the year using a currency of notional 'purple pounds'. The accounts have been prepared on the basis of this notional trading, on the basis that all 'purple pound' receipts or payments are immediately distributed to or injected by the MOD. (Defence Research Agency)

The future of creative accounting

The Accounting Standards Board is working hard to develop standards to eliminate practices which might be considered doubtful, and it uses the Urgent Issues Task Force abstracts to help in this process. FRS 5 (Reporting the substance of transactions) should be a notable help.

However, there are many creative brains among the accountants preparing accounts. Whatever gaps the ASB plugs, it seems likely that more will continue to be created. The only way to prevent this would be to move back to a very prescribed form of accounting, perhaps cash accounting, with all its limitations. Accruals accounting does allow judgements in the interests of substance over form, but opinions may then differ on whether particular judgements are appropriate. The outside observer therefore needs to:

- read the notes and accounting policies carefully
- watch carefully for significant changes in figures from year to year and identify the reasons for them
- take even more care if the auditor's report is anything other than 'true and fair.'

References

Samuel Johnson
Letter to Boswell, 30 March 1778
in *Boswells Life*

K H M Naser
Creative Financial Accounting
Prentice Hall, Hemel Hempstead   1993

H M Treasury
Accounting for capital assets : a working draft of guidance
Unpublished   1992

Chapter 12

Accounting systems

The debits are by the window. (*Traditional*)

This chapter is intended to provide a brief explanation of the underlying accounting systems which can be used to produce accruals accounts. It is not essential to an understanding of the other chapters.

The accounting system

The purpose of an accounting system is to provide an orderly way in which the basic information about day-to-day financial transactions can be collected, summarised and organised to produce the final accounts. The system should not only provide everything which the organisation's management wants, but should also satisfy the needs of the auditors. The key stages are set out in Figure 12.1. Each of the stages will now be explained briefly in turn.

Raw data

The raw data must be kept in respect of transactions as they occur for accruals purposes. Copy delivery notes and goods received notes are essential to track movements in and out. Time records will be needed if there is a substantial service operation with work in progress. The records relating to cash cannot be ignored. It is possible to keep only this basic information, and after the year end prepare a set of accounts. This will satisfy the requirements to produce such accounts, and could be audited, but will provide very little information for management during the course of the year.

Books of prime entry

The books of prime entry represent the first time a transaction is recorded. Day books keep a record of all sales and expenses invoices.

Journal

The journal is used for transactions which cannot go through a day book. This may be for depreciation (there is no invoice for depreciation) and for corrections, as for example, when a payment for wages had been incorrectly charged to the VAT account. The journal provides a full record of such items, with explanations.

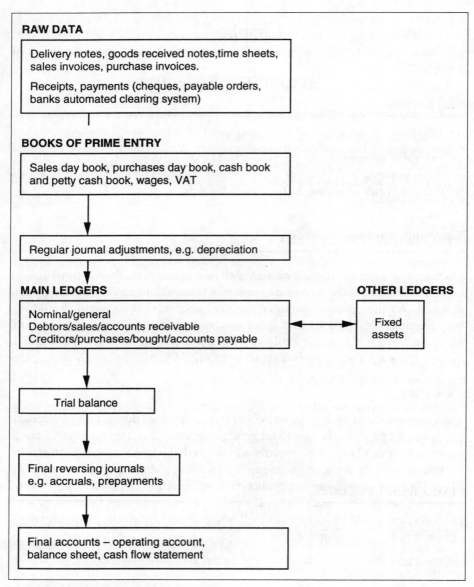

Figure 12.1 Manual accounting systems.

Ledgers

There are different terms in use to refer to approximately the same ledgers. Debtors/sales/accounts receivable ledgers keep track of customers, how much we have sold them, how much cash they have paid us, what the net amount of the debtor is. Creditors/purchases/bought/accounts payable does the same for our suppliers - what we have bought from them, and how much we have paid them.

The nominal/general ledger keeps track of the accounts for all the other balance sheet and operating account headings, such as sales, wages, fixed assets, VAT, telephone. It usually has control accounts managing the total of the debtors and creditors.

Trial balance

The trial balance is a list of all the balances on all the accounts in the general ledger, including the total debtors and creditors. A trial balance can be prepared at any point during the accounting period. It is the first stage in drawing up a set of accounts. It will balance because of the principles of double-entry bookkeeping (see below).

Reversing journals

Reversing journals are needed at the end of each accounting period, perhaps monthly but certainly at the year end. They provide the way to include adjustments for accruals and prepayments which have not yet been recorded through the books of a prime entry. An accrual adjustment would increase the expense in the current period, and reduce the expense in the following period when the invoice for both periods is received. Thus an accrual of £500 for one month's telephone would increase this year's charge, but reduce the £1,500 invoice for the quarter to £1,000 charge for the next year.

Prepayments work the other way, in that if 9 out of 12 months' maintenance, costing £2,400 in total, had been prepaid, then the prepayment would reduce this year's cost by £1,800, and increase next year's cost by the same amount.

Fixed asset register

Although the general ledger will contain an account for the total spent on each category of fixed asset, it is likely that an organisation will wish to keep more information. This can be done by setting up a fixed asset register, which can contain information such as:

- type of asset
- purchase cost
- index for revaluation
- revalued amount
- description
- serial number

- location
- cost centre
- date of purchase
- expected life
- residual value
- depreciation rate and method
- grant value
- depreciation
- date of last inspection
- disposal proceeds
- maintenance arrangements.

The fixed asset register can also be used to track items which are of lower value than the threshold for capitalisation in the accounts, the valuable and portable items. It is useful when valuing the fixed assets for the balance sheet, but it also plays a role in safeguarding the assets.

Double entry bookkeeping

There are many books covering this subject in depth, such as Wood 1993. The purpose here is to explain what it is about, not how it works in detail.

Single entry bookkeeping can and does exist. If the diagram in Figure 12.1 were followed down to the stage of books of prime entry, then those could be used to prepare accounts. Every transaction would have been recorded, albeit only once.

Double entry bookkeeping was devised to provide extra information as well as providing a check against mistakes. The system was first described in 1494 by Luca Pacioli, a Franciscan Monk.

The system works by recording every transaction as it affects the following categories:

- income
- expenditure
- assets
- liabilities
- capital.

Every transaction must have two effects, equal and opposite.

Accounts affected

Purchase of stock on credit	Stock	Creditors
Pay cash for stationery	Stationery	Cash
Pay salaries	Salaries (gross)	Cash (net)
		PAYE and NI creditor

Complex transactions can affect more than two accounts, as in the case of the salaries payment. In order to record the effect, each account will be debited or credited by the amount of the transaction. The terms debit and credit have no implication of right and wrong, or good and bad. By convention:

- assets and expenses are debits, and an increase in them will be a debit
- liabilities, income and capital are credits, and an increase in them will be a credit.

(Be careful, though when looking at your own bank statement. This is written from the bank's viewpoint. Your bank statement will say you have a credit or debit balance. A credit balance means that the bank owes you money, and you are their creditor. A debit balance means that you owe the bank money, you are their debtor.)

So if a fixed asset is sold for cash:

- cash gets debited (it increases)
- fixed assets get credited (they decrease.)

If a creditor is paid off:

- we debit the creditor (it reduces)
- we credit the cash (it reduces.)

Once all the transactions for the period have been entered in the books, we can check if the double entry seems right, by taking out a trial balance. This will spot errors such as a credit for £340 and a debit for £430, but it will not spot items in the wrong account, items not entered at all or items entered twice.

A trial balance for Book Selling Enterprises, using the data shown in Chapters 5 and 6, would appear as in Figure 12.2.

For most of these it should be clear why each account is in debit or credit, following the rules that assets and expenses are debits and liabilities, income and capital are credits. The closing stock appears as both because it is an asset on the balance sheet and hence a debit, and it reduces the expense, the cost of sales, on the operating account and thus a credit.

	Debit	Credit
Sales		40,000
Purchases	25,000	
Closing stock	10,000	10,000
Admin expenses	15,000	
Depreciation charge - vehicle	1,000	
- furniture	500	
- leasehold	2,000	
Interest	3,000	
Leasehold premises - cost	40,000	
Leasehold premises - accumulated depreciation		2,000
Vehicle - cost	8,000	
Vehicle - accumulated depreciation		1,000
Furniture - cost	10,000	
Furniture - accumulated depreciation		500
Debtors	40,000	
Bank	27,000	
Creditors		25,000
Accrued interest		3,000
Loan		100,000
	181,500	181,500

Figure 12.2. Book Selling Enterprises – trial balance.

And why are the debits by the window? In days before artificial light, clerks would sit with natural light on their left so that their writing hand did not cast a shadow on the books.

Manual or computerised system

If an organisation is progressing to an accruals accounting system, it would be well advised not to make the move from manual to computerised at the same time. There are many advantages in accounts staff understanding the principles of accruals before making the transition, not least that they will be better informed to make a meaningful input into the choice of system.

A manual system can be adequate for an organisation which is not very large or complex and which does not need sophisticated analysis of information. The House of Lords operated its accounts on a manual system until 1992. There may be advantages in starting by computerising the most complicated part of the system, where the benefits will be greatest, and leaving the rest manual for a while.

If the whole accounting system is to be computerised, this may be done by way of a series of separate, linked computer packages, or by an integrated package (which may be based on a database rather than a traditional accounting system.) There may be constraints if the system has to match the feeder systems of another organisation, perhaps a parent department.

In developing a computer based system, an organisation should try to involve its auditors as early as possible in the process. Most auditors, including the National Audit Office, would rather advise on the suitability and possible problems of a system than turn up to carry out the audit and find that a system had already been installed. They will, nevertheless, be careful to retain a degree of independence to ensure that their final audit is not pre-judged.

References

F Wood
Business Accounting Vol 1 & 2
Pitman, London   1993

Glossary of terms

Accounting policies

The ways the organisation has chosen to apply accounting standards.

Accounting standards

Standards developed by the accountancy profession to improve disclosure and comparability of accounts. These are SSAPs and FRSs.

Accounting period

The period of time for which financial accounts are prepared, usually 12 months.

Accounts receivable

See debtors.

Accounts payable

See creditors.

Accrual

Adjustment to reflect the timing difference between receipt of goods or services and recording of invoice. An accrual increases the cost for the current period to include such items.

Accruals concept

Income is accounted for when earned, and costs when incurred. Also known as the matching concept, as income and costs are matched to the relevant period.

Accumulated depreciation

The depreciation charged to date on a fixed asset, or category of fixed asset.

Amortisation

The fall in value of a lease or an intangible asset over time.

Asset

Anything of value owned or controlled by an organisation as a result of past transactions or events. Assets may be current or fixed.

Audit

See external audit, internal audit.

Bad debts
The debts owed to an organisation which are regarded as uncollectable and are written off.

Balance sheet
A statement of the financial position of an organisation at a given date, showing the net worth. It discloses the book value of the assets, liabilities, capital and reserves.

Bookkeeping
The analysis, classification and recording of financial transactions in books of account.

Book value
The amount at which an asset is recorded in the accounts, cost (current or historical) less accumulated depreciation.

Capital
The owners' interest in the organisation, it equals assets less liabilities. Also known as equity or net worth.

Capital asset
See fixed asset.

Capital charge
A charge to local authority revenue accounts to reflect the cost of fixed assets used in the provision of services. It consists of depreciation and interest.

Capital expenditure
Expenditure on acquiring or improving fixed assets.

Cash flow statement
A financial statement which shows where the cash came from and where it went in the period.

Cash flow forecast
An internal management document forecasting the movements in cash in the future.

Commitment accounting
A method of accounting which recognises costs and liabilities as soon as orders are placed with suppliers. This is earlier than accruals, which recognises costs when the goods or services are received.

Communicated costs
See notional costs.

Conservatism
Excessive prudence, where net assets are deliberately understated.

Consistency concept
Like items should be treated in the same way from one period to the next.

Contingent liability
A liability where the amount and likelihood of payment are uncertain, so it is not provided for in the balance sheet, only disclosed.

Cost of sales/cost of goods sold
The cost of producing the goods or services which were sold in the period.

Creditors
Suppliers and others to whom the organisation owes money. Americanised as accounts payable.

Current assets
Assets that are part of the trading cycle, and which will turn into cash, usually within 12 months of the balance sheet date. Examples are stock, work in progress, debtors, bank and cash.

Current liabilities
Liabilities which have to be paid within 12 months of the balance sheet date e.g. creditors, bank overdrafts.

Debtors
Customers or others who owe money to the business. Americanised as accounts receivable.

Deferred tax
Tax attributable to timing differences between results as computed for tax purposes and results as stated in the accounts, payable sometime in the future.

Deficit
The outcome where costs exceed income for the period. Loss.

Depreciation
The fall in value of a fixed asset as a result of use, physical deterioration, obsolescence or the passage of time.

Double-entry bookkeeping

A system of bookkeeping which reflects the dual aspect of each transaction by means of debit and credit entries in the books of account.

Equity

See capital.

Exceptional item

Material item which derives from events or transactions that fall within the ordinary activities of the organisation. Ordinary activities include the effects on the organisation of any event in the various environments in which it operates, including the political, regulatory, economic and geographic environments, irrespective of the frequency or unusual nature of the events.

External audit

The independent examination of, and expression of opinion on, the financial statements of an organisation.

Extraordinary item

Material item possessing a high degree of abnormality which arises from events or transactions which fall outside the ordinary activities of the organisation and which is not expected to recur.

Fixed asset

Asset acquired for use in the organisation, not for resale in the normal course of business. Examples are land and buildings, equipment, computers. Also known as capital asset.

FRSs - financial reporting standards

Accounting standards issued by the Accounting Standards Board.

GAAP - generally accepted accounting practice

Accounting practice which conforms with the requirements of the Companies Act 1985 and Accounting Standards.

General fund

An alternative name for capital and reserves.

Going concern concept

The values of items in the accounts are calculated on the assumption that the organisation will continue in operation for the foreseeable future, rather than sale value or break-up value.

Gross surplus

The surplus achieved on selling goods and services before taking into account expenses. It equals turnover less cost of sales.

Income and expenditure account

See operating account.

Intangible assets

Assets which are not of a physical nature, e.g. patents, software.

Internal audit

An independent appraisal within an organisation which operates as a service to management by measuring and evaluating the effectiveness of the internal control system.

Internal control system

The whole system of controls, financial and otherwise, established by management in order to carry on the operations of the organisation in an orderly and efficient manner, ensure adherence to management policies, safeguard the assets and secure as far as possible the completeness and accuracy of the records.

Inventory

A list of items. This may be a detailed list of fixed assets, usually without cost and depreciation information, or a stock count.

Investments

Monetary holdings or fixed assets which are intended to produce interest, income, profit, growth or other benefit.

Liability

The obligation to confer future economic benefit as a result of past transactions or events.

Loss

See deficit.

Management accounting

The preparation and presentation of accounting and control information to support management, be it in strategic planning or day-to-day control. Management accounting information is usually a combination of accruals or cash accounting and non-financial data such as units or hours.

Matching concept
See accruals concept.

Materiality
An item is material if its omission or misstatement would affect the view taken by a reasonable user of the accounts.

Memorandum trading account
A document similar to an operating account, prepared to help set prices and monitor results of a public sector service which charges fees.

Net surplus
Gross surplus, less expenses in selling, distribution and administration.

Non-cash costs
See notional costs.

Notional costs
Costs which are not reflected by cash transactions affecting the organisation, but are costs incurred elsewhere on behalf of the organisation. Examples in the government sector are insurance and interest on capital. Sometimes referred to as non-cash costs or communicated costs.

Operating account
A financial statement which shows the results for the period, with income and costs and the net surplus or deficit. Also known as income and expenditure account, profit and loss account or revenue account.

Post balance sheet event
A significant event, favourable or unfavourable, which occurs between the balance sheet date and the date the accounts are approved by the organisation's management. It may require disclosure or adjustment in the accounts.

Prepayments
Expenditure on goods and services for future benefit, which is to be charged to the cost of future operations.

Prior year adjustment
Restating the results of previous years as a result of changes in accounting policies or to correct fundamental errors.

Profit
See surplus.

Profit and loss account
See operating account.

Provisions
Amounts written off or retained to provide for renewals, fall in value of assets, or for a known liability whose extent cannot be precisely determined.

Prudence concept
Liabilities and costs are anticipated, but assets and gains are not.

Reserves
Undistributed surpluses.

Resource accounting
A type of accruals accounting under development for government departments.

Revaluation reserve
A reserve reflecting the upwards (or downwards) revaluation of fixed assets from their original purchase cost.

Revenue
The income of the organisation.

Revenue expenditure
Expenditure which is in order to obtain revenue (e.g. salaries) or to maintain operating capacity (e.g. repairs).

SSAPs - statements of standard accounting practice
Accounting standards adopted and amended by the Accounting Standards Board.

Stock
Goods purchased for resale, consumable stores, raw materials and finished goods.

Surplus
The excess of income over costs. Profit.

Tangible assets
Assets which are physical in nature, e.g. stock, vehicles.

Trial balance
A list of all the balances in the books of account, on one date.

True and fair view
One which does not mislead a user of the accounts.

Turnover
The value of services and goods sold by the organisation.

Working capital
Current assets less current liaiblities, the capital available to conduct day-to-day operations of the organisation.

Work in progress
For service organisations, the value of direct costs, labour and overheads of work started before the balance sheet date, but not yet completed and invoiced. For manufacturing organisations, the value of materials, labour and overheads in partly completed products.

Index

Supply Estimate, 8, 17.

Surplus, 19, 36, 45, 47, 48, 62, 63, 65, 67, 68, 70, 72, 78, 79, 83, 106, 107, 132-135, 143, 145, 146, 167.

Surrey County Council, 96-102, 122.

T

Tangible assets, 167.

Tate Gallery, 103.

Trading Accounts, 36.

Trading funds, 4, 9, 10, 30, 32, 33, 62,65, 81, 83, 108, 132, 135, 137, 149, 150.

Treasury, 12, 20, 32, 39, 53, 70, 75, 76, 81, 83, 85-92, 94, 108, 131, 132, 137, 149.

Trial balance, 154, 155, 157, 158, 167.

True and fair view, 22, 76, 80, 87, 96, 105, 119, 123, 124, 167.

Turnover, 47, 48, 78, 79, 106, 107, 133, 138, 144, 145, 168.

U

Unit cost, 136,137.

University, 14, 15, 75, 103, 104, 128.

University of Manchester, 15.

University of Oxford, 14, 15.

University of St Andrews, 58, 104.

Urgent Issues Task Force, 79, 151.

Users of accounts, 2.

V

Valuation of fixed assets, 52, 53, 93, 148, 149.

Value added tax (VAT), 57, 59, 68, 77, 78, 153, 155.

Value for money audit, 116, 128, 129.

Vehicle Inspectorate, 4, 9, 53, 54, 56, 61, 135-137.

Victoria and Albert Museum, 15.

W

Wilton Park Conference Centre, 9.

Winchester College, 14.

Work in progress, 56, 57, 86, 140, 148, 150, 153, 168.

Working capital, 72, 168.